The Little Book of

loose
women

Also By
loose
women

Girls' Night In

Here Come the Girls

The Little Book of
loose
women

HODDER &
STOUGHTON

First published in Great Britain in 2010 by Hodder & Stoughton
An Hachette UK company
Illustrations © Marjorie Dumortier

1

Loose Women is an ITV Studios Ltd Production
Copyright © ITV Studios Ltd 2010
Licensed by ITV Global Entertainment Ltd

A CIP catalogue record for this title is available from the British Library.

ISBN 978 1 444 70018 3

Typeset in Adobe Caslon by Hewer Text UK Ltd, Edinburgh
Printed and bound by Clays Ltd, St Ives plc

Hodder & Stoughton policy is to use papers that are natural, renewable and recyclable products and made from wood grown in sustainable forests. The logging and manufacturing processes are expected to conform to the environmental regulations of the country of origin.

Hodder & Stoughton Ltd
338 Euston Road
London NW1 3BH

www.hodder.co.uk

That's what friends are for!

Contents

Introduction

Get the kettle on, because the Loose Women are back and we've got a whole lot to get off our chests. This may be *The Little Book of Loose Women* but don't fret, we've managed to cram a lot of big personalities into these pint-sized pages, and we'll tell you something for nothing: it was quite a squeeze!

As you might expect from a bunch of women who talk for a living, we've got an opinion about pretty much everything under the sun and we're more than happy to share them with you. What's more, we're not afraid to lay bare our souls if we think it'll help other women who are going through the same things.

And, let me tell you, between us we've been through the lot: love, heartbreak, betrayal, loneliness, bereavement, joy, childbirth and Botox. We've had holiday romances, alfresco sex and celebrity crushes, declared war on wrinkles, on diets and on the dreaded man flu. In fact, you could fill a whole library with our wise words and silly asides, but who'd have time to read all that? We know that you're run off your feet as it is! That's why we decided to put together this little book of all our best bits for your reading pleasure.

Now if we were putting together the perfect man, there'd be a heck of a lot of arguments. Denise would want a bit of rough. Coleen would just take Ronaldo and rough him up a bit. But eventually we might come up with someone with Enrique Iglesias' eyes, David Beckham's bum and Simon Cowell's power. Likewise, when we put this book together we decided to throw in a bit of Sherrie's quirkiness, a touch of Lynda's no-nonsense outlook and a dash of Carol's dirty humour. We wanted to let Jane let rip, Lesley get frank and Lisa lay it on the line. So that's exactly what we did, and we hope you enjoy reading the book as much as we enjoyed writing it.

As fans of the show will know, we're not famed for holding back, and in *The Little Book of Loose Women* we've really lived up to our reputation. As you'll see, we hold forth on all the topics dearest to our hearts: men, motherhood, manners, modern Britain and whether or not we can pull off wearing a mini-skirt without looking like mutton dressed as lamb. We'll show you why Andrea thinks that men are like dogs (they just need the right sort of training!), what Kate really thinks about man boobs, and we'll argue the toss over the rights and wrongs of everything from little white lies to cosmetic surgery.

When all's said and done, much as we enjoy a bit of banter and heated debate, we all respect each other's views, however wild and wacky they may seem. After all, how boring would it be if we all agreed on everything?

We hope that with *The Little Book of Loose Women* we've put together a small but perfectly formed treat for you to enjoy. But as they say, the proof of the pudding's in the tasting, so what are you waiting for? Get stuck in!

Mothers and Motherhood

☆ ☆ ☆

As much as it pains us to admit it, it turns out that some-times mothers really do know best. That dress *was* too tight. That boy *was* a ne'er-do-well. And the world didn't end because he copped off with some floozy from down the street. It's a good thing too that we're finally giving our poor mums proper credit, since we seem to be turning into them at a terrifying rate! Whether you have your own brood of snotty little angels or you're smugly child-free, I guarantee there'll come a day when you'll sigh, shake your head, and say in all seriousness: 'Oh well. Plenty more fish in the sea.'

* * *

Baby talk

When I gave birth, I felt like a supermum. I felt like I was the only woman who had ever given birth. I wanted a podium, the National Anthem and a medal.   *Coleen*

I have got slight baby phobia, to the point where my friends don't even bother to tell me when they've had their babies anymore. It's not that I'm not interested, but I'm just not interested!   *Carol*

I had Beau at thirty-five and even then I don't think I was mature enough. I wasn't even mature enough to check the test you pee on to find out if you're pregnant. I was so scared that I got Paul to go and check it, so he knew I was pregnant before I did!   *Lisa*

* * *

Sam couldn't help but feel a bit left out.
A 36-hour labour and she didn't even get a cuddly toy.

First moments

I don't think anyone can explain the fear that you feel from
the moment your baby is born and they hand it to you. It's
terrifying when you go home for the first time and you're left
on your own. Shane Junior was a nightmare to get to sleep and
when he finally started sleeping, I'd be so relieved. But then
I'd start listening for his breaths and worrying. Is he breath-
ing? I'd take the blankets off to check and he'd start crying
again! And I'd think, Oh God! Here we go again!   *Coleen*

When Keeley was born, they put her face next to
mine. I heard the midwife say, 'Now that's true love.'
And it's been true love ever since.   *Sherrie*

Those first moments as you're leaving the hospital with
your baby in her carry-cot are very strange. You've
got a baby there and you don't quite know how it got
there! You think someone's going to come up to you
and say, 'What are you doing with that baby?'   *Lisa*

☆☆ ☆☆ ☆☆ ☆☆

When I was in labour, I tried to strangle my ex-husband when he came to stand beside me. I grabbed him by the neck and wouldn't let go. Sadly, he got away!

Sherrie

☆☆ ☆☆ ☆☆ ☆☆

Pram rage

What is it about mums with new babies? Why do they suddenly think they have right of way everywhere they go? You know, when you're walking down the road and there's a mum pushing a pushchair with a baby; there's not much space in the road and they walk in a straight line, expecting you to get out of the way. What is that?   *Carol*

I get pram rage sometimes, because people don't get out of my way! It's actually far more difficult to change direction when you've got a pram than it is for someone sauntering along to side-step and walk by.   *Andrea*

I don't complain about children. All I complain about is children making a horrible noise in restaurants, and buggies everywhere. You can't get round the super-market because there are so many of them! All push-chairs should be left outside the shop.   *Carol*

* * *

Kid-free zone

I really hate the way people tell other people how to be. Women with kids, for instance, always say, 'Why haven't you got any children?' Like I'm the weirdo! Why do women without children always have to justify their decision?   *Carol*

'Shopping is sooo much more efficient this way,' said
Liz as the mums skipped off into the supermarket.

I think of myself as child-free and not child-less. Not having children has become more of a lifestyle choice for some women.   *Carol*

* * *

Supermums

☆☆ ☆☆ ☆☆ ☆☆

My mother has never let me down, in any shape or form. She's my best friend, my confidante and I would always turn to her in a crisis.

Jane

☆☆ ☆☆ ☆☆ ☆☆

There's nothing like a good old chinwag with your mum.

Looking at pictures is the way I remember people, along with the memories that I'll always have in my heart. I've got a lovely picture in my bedroom of my mum with Ciara.   *Coleen*

If my daughter got married, I would never interfere. I would have nothing to do with the wedding whatsoever. The only things I would be interested in are where it was, what she was wearing, the bridesmaids, the page-boy suits, the groom, the balloons, the flowers and the invitations. But nothing else!   *Sherrie*

My mum's a bit like Mrs Doubtfire, the typical old-fashioned mum really. She can cook, she can bake and she makes everything from scratch. I'm very lucky really, because I've got this wonderful mum who is a wonderful housekeeper as well. It helps me a great deal. Her cooking is second to none and I love her shepherd's pie.   *Jane*

My mum was a farmer's wife. She worked hard all day, and I mean hard labour, but at 4pm or 4.30pm, you'd walk into a warm room where there was toast and jam and a cup of tea. Why would you want to go out then, after that? I truly think that if young men could come home to that it would stop a lot of trouble. Nurturing has gone out the window a bit, because everybody's chasing the dream and everybody's gone out to work. I know it's necessary, but to me one of the single biggest factors in the breakdown of teenage society is not having anybody to come home to. The classic thing with teenage children is that they don't want to talk to you, but if you're not there, they miss you! *Lynda*

When my marriage ended, I wrote a song for my mum called 'The Hand That Leads Me'. It's about how she took my hand, like she did when I was six, and said, 'We'll get through this together.' She led me through the darkest time of my life and I'll always be grateful that I had her around. Sometimes she didn't even have to say anything: she just put her hand out and touched my knee and that was enough comfort. *Jane*

* * *

Turning into your mother

☆☆ ☆☆ ☆☆ ☆☆

Everybody says it and it's true: you don't really appreciate your mum until you have kids.

Andrea

☆☆ ☆☆ ☆☆ ☆☆

I've turned into my mum! I hear myself saying things like 'Have you eaten?' *Jane*

My mum, God rest her soul, truly believed that if you gave people enough love, it would be returned. That's not always the case, but it's a good way to live. *Lynda*

My mother still cooks as if there are about eighteen people to feed. We always say, 'When's the rugby team turning up?' I have tried so many times to say,

'There are only two of us,' or 'There are only three of us.' It's the mothering instinct, isn't it?   *Jane*

* * *

Spoil 'em rotten

People have always accused me of spoiling Keeley. But you know what? She's turned out to be the most beautiful human being, so I must have done something right. I don't think I've spoiled her. I've just loved her beyond the point of duty. Loving someone a lot can't be wrong, and it's the same with my grandson Oliver.   *Sherrie*

You can't just let kids think that they can be given everything for nothing. We didn't get pocket money, but we still did all the chores. One of our chores was to lay the table and clear the table. We used to put a second tablecloth over the table-cloth, to keep it clean. We thought it was hilarious to fold it up with all the crumbs in it, so that when she took it out to put on the table, the crumbs would tumble out! We'd really get told off.   *Carol*

It's your responsibility as a mother to send your son off to the woman he'll share a life and home with, knowing that actually homes don't run themselves. 'It's not a hotel, mate.' It's really important.   *Kate*

* * *

Letting go

I'm more fearful now for my sons, who are older, than I am for Ciara, because Ciara's eight and still under my control. I know where she is, who she's with and what she's doing. The boys are now out in the big bad world on their own.

'See you later, Mum, I'm just going out,' Shane says. I say, 'OK, I love you,' and I give him a hug. When he gets to the car, I run out and say, 'I love you!' and hug him again.

'You've just done that in the kitchen,' he'll say.
'I know, but it might be the last time (sob!).'
'But I'm only going to the garage!'   *Coleen*

My mum clucks over me, but she also knows that
I need my space, so she's a perfect partner to have
in the house. She goes up to her end and I come
down to my end and we just meet in the middle
for meals and a chat. It's perfect, absolutely perfect.
It's funny, because I assume that everybody has
the kind of relationship that I've got with my
mum, and of course a lot of people don't.   *Jane*

If you're lecturing your child about something, it's much
more constructive if you say, 'Look, I went through
that when I was younger and this was how I dealt with
it and it was a bad way of dealing with it.'   *Coleen*

★ ★ ★

Mum's the word

I'm very open with my children. I don't sit them down
and tell them everything I've done in my past, but if
they come to me with any problems or ask me a question, I always answer as honestly as possible. I think
it's because when I was younger, my parents didn't
answer any questions. My mum's answer to everything was, 'Don't worry, you'll find out soon enough.'
My children also know where the line is. I don't want
to just be their best friend, because I'm their parent
as well. They can come to me with anything, but
they can't always expect me to say, 'That's OK, son.'
Sometimes they'll get the lecture from hell.   *Coleen*

My mother is my best friend. I can tell her anything and
she has confided in me too. I know an awful lot about
her and she knows absolutely everything about me.
It's a trust we've got. She's the one person I can go to
and say, 'I don't know how I'm going to handle this.' If

she's been through it, she'll say, 'Well, I did it this way.' Or, 'Don't do it that way, because I did that.' *Jane*

I keep schtum when it comes to my sons' girlfriends. Whatever I said, they would do the opposite. Anyway, mothers never take into account sexual chemistry. My mother might have said, 'That's a nice boy!' when in fact he was horrible. It could be a lawyer or a doctor or someone with lots of money, but if you don't fancy them, there's not a lot of point, is there? *Lynda*

* * *

Mum as fashion guru

My mum used to make most of our clothes! I protested at loads of things, but as my mum laughingly recalls, 'You were always the one that we could talk round.' I remember I took part in a public speaking competition and my mum said, 'Why don't you wear that jumper that Granny knitted you? She'll be so proud.' Well, my mum used to perm my hair and I had acne at the time, so there's a photograph of me in the local paper looking absolutely hideous, with a home perm and spots, wearing a mint green jumper with brown flowers on it! I look at it now and think, 'No wonder I had no boyfriends!' *Andrea*

My mum used to buy me some very strange things, normally from second-hand shops. I had some shocking flowery dresses when flowery dresses weren't in anymore. She'd say, 'It looks fine on you,' and I'd be thinking, 'No, it looks hideous.' *Coleen*

When Sharon invited her mum to her hen do,
this was not what she'd bargained for...

Style

☆ ☆ ☆

While there's a lot to be said for slumming around the house in a pair of trackie bottoms and fluffy slippers, sometimes a girl has to pull out all the stops. Getting glammed up doesn't necessarily mean stopping traffic or scaring children with yards of goosepimply flesh. It can mean something as simple as swapping your granny pants for lacy little numbers – even if the only time other folk get to see your smalls is when you hang them out to dry. Don't forget that with the current economic climate, shopping has become practically a national duty. Ready your cash registers, Britain, because the *Loose Women* are coming . . .

* * *

Glam it up

☆☆ ☆☆ ☆☆ ☆☆

If in doubt, get some sequins and a bit of feather on it.

Jane

☆☆ ☆☆ ☆☆ ☆☆

Feathers scream old-fashioned glamour, I think. When I think of Fred Astaire and Ginger Rogers, when I think of Marlene Dietrich and when I think of Busby Barclay, I think of feathers, which is why I wear a lot of ostrich feathers. *Lesley*

Attitudes change. Once upon a time, you saw Elizabeth Taylor, Joan Crawford and Bette Davis in beautiful mink coats and you just thought it was the ultimate in glamour. There was always a sense that you'd made it if you had a mink coat. But it's totally different today. *Jane*

I hate all that girly baby pink stuff. It's a cliché. Girls are supposed to like pink, which is perhaps why I don't like it. I would look like a trannie in baby pink. *Carol*

* * *

Dressing for men

My husband likes me in pencil skirts and tailored suits, but I'm not going to play Twister with a six-year-old in a pencil skirt. It might be good for him, but it won't be good for me. *Coleen*

My husband is never happier than if I'm in a little cardigan. He finds very unusual things attractive. Whereas some men prefer silk, my husband prefers flannelette. He likes me to wear it anytime, but particularly in bed. *Lesley*

If you've been single for a while, you tend to walk around the house in the cosiest, comfiest stuff. I wear the same tracksuit bottoms and top every single day when I'm at home. But having a boyfriend snaps you out of that. I wouldn't dream of putting it on now. All my single slouchy clothes have been hidden in the cupboard.   *Carol*

★ ★ ★

Over-exposure

I flash less flesh now, because there are a lot less attractive parts of me to flash!   *Lisa*

☆☆ ☆☆ ☆☆ ☆☆

I don't like my trousers to show my knickers. I don't know about anybody else, but as soon as I put a proper pair of knickers on, I've got four backsides.

Jane

☆☆ ☆☆ ☆☆ ☆☆

I think there's a time and a place to dress provoca-
tively. If I was having a dinner and someone turned
up at my house with all their bits hanging out and got
their boobs out in front of my husband, I'd be bloomin'
annoyed! It's cheating, because the rest of us have to
rely on our intellect and sense of humour. I wouldn't
wave my boobs around in front of her husband. *Lisa*

★ ★ ★

Bridget Jones pants

Pull-it-all-in pants are not sexy. My worry is that a guy
will see me in a tight mini dress across the room and say,
'Wow, look at the figure on her!' So you pull, you go back
to the room, you take it off and it all falls out! *Zoe*

Taking off a corset can be like a sausage
coming out of its skin! *Kate*

You should make the most of what you've got, because once you've got them back to your place, I don't think they care. It's like a carrot – and they're the donkey. They look at you dressed up and think, 'Whoo, I've got to have a bit of that.' By the time you get back and take it all off, I'm absolutely certain that most blokes couldn't care less if you've got a bit of flesh under there. I really don't think they're that bothered.   *Carol*

I think you'd need counselling if you went in my knicker drawer. It's not racy and sexy; it's grey and big and doesn't co-ordinate at all! I have my nice pants for when I'm going out in the evening – just one pair – and I think that maybe at the end of the night, Ray and I will, you know! But the rest of the time, it's big Bridget Jones pants, and now I've lost weight, it's big Bridget Jones baggy pants!   *Coleen*

When I was married, it was all big knickers, but when I was single, I had lovely underwear. It seemed a bit of a waste, because I was the only one who saw it. Apart from the people next door, of course, when it was hanging on the line! *Jane*

★ ★ ★

Killer heels

I've got so many high-heeled boots that my mother goes mad. 'Do you honestly need another pair of black boots?' she'll ask. Of course I do! I'm going to keep wearing boots with high heels as long as I can, because one day I'll think, I can't wear these anymore; my feet are killing me! It probably won't be that long, either! *Jane*

High heels give you good posture and make you stand beautifully, by pulling your back up and your tummy in. My mother walks elegantly in high heels, but I don't. I fall off them. I'm not good with heights! *Sherrie*

Clare had developed an uncanny ability to spot
a gorgeous pair of shoes from fifty paces.

I always used to put on high heels for *Loose Women*. It was a confidence thing; they made me feel I could rule the world.   *Carol*

* * *

Suffering for fashion

☆☆ ☆☆ ☆☆ ☆☆

I can only do elegant for about an hour and then I want to take everything off, scratch myself and put my comfy clothes back on.
Coleen

☆☆ ☆☆ ☆☆ ☆☆

I won't freeze for fashion, absolutely not! I couldn't care less if I turned up at a premiere in a Parka or an anorak, because I can't bear being cold. It's more miserable than being hungry or tired for me.   *Carol*

It's illegal to wear a coat in Newcastle. I'm sure that you actually get arrested if you walk along the Newcastle quayside wearing a coat. It happens in every major city, but in Newcastle it's legendary. The colder the weather, the skimpier the costumes. I've seen girls standing at the bus stop on New Year's Eve in the middle of a blizzard wearing sleeveless tops, with corn-beef legs and a fag out.   *Denise*

* * *

Looking sexy

If nightwear looks contrived, then it's not sexy, in my opinion.   *Lisa*

A corseted, boned dress can look really great, but this trend of wearing corsets as outerwear is horrible. Your boobs are under your chin, you've got back fat pouring out and yet you strut around thinking you look sexy! Well, you're not. You're just like a pair of old knees!   *Kate*

Most people don't look sexy in knitwear. I don't
think woolly jumpers can ever really be sexy
unless you're Julia Roberts in front of a fire in
a movie, with nothing else on.   *Carol*

To make the best of yourself, you need to identify your
best bits and worst bits, and be really honest with yourself. For instance, I've never gone out in hipsters and
a top showing off my midriff, because I know that
would just make people sick, including myself.
I saw so many people walking round town when that
look was in fashion, and it didn't suit even some of
the young girls, because they had rolls of fat bulging out. You just think, NO! I know it's in fashion, but only if you're a size eight!   *Coleen*

★ ★ ★

Shop 'til you drop

I never regret buying things. I'm always glad that I bought something because it means that I don't get up the next day wishing I'd got it. That's a worse feeling!   *Jane*

Shopping is difficult for blokes! It doesn't come naturally to them, does it?   *Carol*

Men just don't seem to get it right, do they? Especially when it comes to underwear. They don't seem to know your size, and it's always two sizes too small.   *Jane*

Diet and Fitness

☆ ☆ ☆

The papers are always whinging about Fast Food Britain, but the other side of it is all those poor women who've been on a diet practically their whole adult lives. Atkins, liquid detox, cabbage soup: they all seem designed to make your life a misery and transform you into a human methane machine. Give it up, ladies, it never works! And why should you deny yourself when your partner is busy adding to his beer belly? Someday soon his boobs will be bigger than yours! So don't feel bad if you prefer the telly to the treadmill. You're in good company – ours!

* * *

Belinda was having second thoughts about the personal
trainer. 'You have got to be kidding me,' she wheezed,
'three times round the park for a flaming jaffa cake?!'

Generation fat

If the parents aren't living healthily, then what hope is there for the kids? I have seen overweight kids out in the street and normally following behind them are Mr and Mrs Overweight. It makes you want to say, 'Step back from the cake, fatty!' *Coleen*

I think a lot of kids now who have self-esteem issues inherit them from their parents. Paranoid mothers who are always on diets are bound to pass their body image issues to their daughters, aren't they? *Carol*

How dare men make their other half feel insecure about their looks as they get steadily paunchier? You want to say to them, 'Go away, mate, and sort yourself out before you tell me what to do!' *Lynda*

★ ★ ★

Battle of the sexes

☆☆ ☆☆ ☆☆ ☆☆

**I don't like to be with someone
thinner than me, because I like to
eat pies and have pizza.**

Jane

☆☆ ☆☆ ☆☆ ☆☆

When you're in a relationship, you do have a bit of a
duty to your partner not to put on a lot of weight. You
see men with man boobs everywhere on the beach! Still,
it would be handy to be going out with somebody who
had man boobs if you didn't have any. You could both go
for surgery at the same time and have a swap.   *Carol*

It's not about how you look, it's how you are and
how you feel about somebody. So I could get along
with man boobs. Last year Darren watched my body

40

expand hugely because I brought our child into the world, but it didn't stop him loving me.   *Kate*

☆☆ ☆☆ ☆☆ ☆☆

I wouldn't like a man to have bigger boobs than me.

Sherrie

☆☆ ☆☆ ☆☆ ☆☆

Defying gravity

How did the rhyme go at school? 'I must, I must, improve my bust. The bigger, the better, the tighter the sweater, the boys depend on us!'   *Andrea*

When I'm doing my three-second jog back from school to my house, if there are traffic lights and the cars stop, I walk, because I can't bear people looking at that 'two ferrets in a sack' thing. Do you know what I mean?   *Denise*

I like to walk, because I believe that if you run
after a certain age, all it does is give gravity
a giant helping hand, by forcing everything down, down, down! *Carol*

Diet madness

I've done loads of crash diets over the years and
they work in the short term because you're not
putting the same amount of food into your mouth.
But the problem is that once you stop dieting and
eat one slice of toast, the weight's back on plus
a stone. Also, you spend your whole time waiting for the diet to come to an end, so that you can
eat again. So what's the point, really? *Coleen*

'Of course I don't begrudge my family their pizza,' thought
Sally, miserably contemplating her bowl of green mush.

☆☆ ☆☆ ☆☆ ☆☆

The word diet doesn't really enter my vocabulary.

Carol

☆☆ ☆☆ ☆☆ ☆☆

Everyone says, 'Isn't it marvellous in the summer? You just want a salad.' Rubbish! I want carbohydrates all year round! Then they say, 'Isn't it marvellous in the winter? You can have carbohydrates because you need something warming.' It's all crap! I can put on weight anytime, summer or winter.   *Lynda*

Women will always want to be half a stone lighter.   *Denise*

If I even think about going on a diet, I instantly start craving chocolate, so there's no point to dieting for me. Feeling deprived just makes you want something even more and life's too short to feel you're missing out.   *Andrea*

★ ★ ★

Who needs a man when you can have cake?

The divorce diet

The best weight loss for me was divorce. Fantastic.
I lost about twelve stone of ugly flesh! *Jane*

I never got the divorce diet. I just ate through
the divorce. I ate through the tears. *Coleen*

★ ★ ★

Gym bunny

My bouts of exercising are very intermittent. My
trainer says I'm the worst client she's ever had because
I never go training with her. I just say in a whisper, 'Let's have a glass of wine instead ...' *Denise*

Food and Drink

☆ ☆ ☆

Sex is all well and good, but sometimes you just fancy a cup of tea – or a big glass of bubbly and some gooey chocolate creation that will melt in your mouth and leave you desperate for more ... Sorry, we got a little carried away there! As every Loose Woman knows, there's far more to food and drink than convenience and calorie content. Whether it's wine to get you in a frisky mood or a fancy meal that'll leave you smiling for days, there's every excuse for a bit of self-indulgence now and then. At least, that's our line, and we're sticking to it!

* * *

Just the one . . .

What really annoys me are celebrities who give up drinking. You know, they've had their fun and then they say, 'Oh, it's so much better being sober,' and start judging other people. Yeah, I'm fifty, I go out and get absolutely drunk as a skunk, but I don't care. I don't judge them for being sober. I don't say, 'Oh my God, what a ridiculous thing to be sober. How tragic is that?' I would never say that!   *Carol*

I like a bargain, so if my drinks are included in the price of a meal or night out, it is within my rights to drink my own body weight. If it's in, drink it. That's what I say.   *Jane*

☆☆ ☆☆ ☆☆ ☆☆

I like a drink. If I had never drunk, I would probably never have had sex.

Carol

☆☆ ☆☆ ☆☆ ☆☆

Does alcohol make lovemaking more fun? If I have a drink, I either go to sleep or I forget what I'm doing. My mind wanders a bit and then I can't get myself focused on what I'm supposed to be doing. I think, 'That ceiling might need doing.' I lose concentration very easily. *Jane*

Sometimes you need to have a drink to get yourself in the zone, but you can't keep doing it. In the beginning, you've got a full face of make-up on and your hair looks fabulous, but you have to get to the point where you reveal the true you, without the hair, without the make-up and without the drink – and that's when they need a drink! *Lisa*

★ ★ ★

The morning after

If you feel a bit ropey in the morning, a sauna is the best cure for a hangover. I would also recommend drinking two pints of warm water mixed with orange juice

– three quarters water to one quarter orange juice. That, and a sauna, sorts me out in the morning. *Carol*

The problem with Mark and I is that I always end up getting drunker than him. It's because there's an age difference of twenty years between us: when I was twenty-seven I could drink all night and I still wouldn't fall over, whereas it's different now. *Carol*

* * *

Sex and food

☆☆ ☆☆ ☆☆ ☆☆

Men like something to grab hold of. Also, if a woman's got curves, a man knows he's going to get a pie when he gets in. It's the way to a man's heart, don't forget!

Jane

☆☆　☆☆　☆☆　☆☆

If the world was coming to an end, would I rather eat or have sex? Take a guess! I don't get pleasure from gorging on food and I do get a lot of pleasure from you-know-what. Why would you want to stuff yourself and feel sick when you're just about to die? I don't really understand why people would feel the need to eat just before they die. I would have sex up until the very last minute. How can the pleasure of the pastry be greater than the pleasure of the flesh? There's no contest for me.　*Carol*

★　★　★

Partying

☆ ☆ ☆

After a drink or two, the three most beautiful words in the English language are: 'Let's have another!' While we've all got issues with tolerance levels and peaking too early (oo-er, missus!) there's still nothing better than a night on the town with the girls for going wild and forgetting the day-to-day grind. Who has time to worry about housework or narky supervisors when the wine's flowing, the music's pumping and you're dancing like a thing possessed? Come on, ladies, time to show those young whippersnappers how it should be done . . .

* * *

'Like a virgin, touched for the very first tiiiiime'

Letting loose

I'm trying to train myself to recognise the moment when I've had enough to drink. The other night I was in a restaurant with a couple of friends and after we'd had a couple of bottles of wine, I was sitting there, thinking, 'Ooh, this is the moment when I should really go home.' But I was wishing one of them would say, 'Let's get another bottle,' because then I'd say, 'Yay!'   *Carol*

I peak too early and Steve gets really cross with me. No, I don't mean like that! I get so excited that I'm going out that we normally have a little drink while we're getting ready and the babysitter arrives. Then we get in the car and once I'm there, I get so excited that I knock a few back. I'll be having a brilliant time and then suddenly I need to go to bed.   *Andrea*

I'm afraid that alcohol plays a big part in my enjoyment of a night out, especially after going two years without it. I'm not talking about messy drunken nights, though. I just love a few glasses of champagne.   *Denise*

I have to say that my tolerance levels are lower now I've given up drinking. I realise that sometimes I drank because I was bored, and now I'm just bored and I go home early. I don't miss it now, although sometimes when we go out, I think, 'If only I could have a glass of champagne to get me chatty!'   *Lynda*

☆☆ ☆☆ ☆☆ ☆☆

It's all about the people: it doesn't matter where you are as long as you're with really good mates.

Andrea

☆☆ ☆☆ ☆☆ ☆☆

I'm too old to party like I do – as Coleen's always pointing out. But I still do it, because I like to party!

I think I'm going to miss something, which is quite pathetic. After a certain amount, I look in the mirror, see somebody thirty years younger and do that flirting with young boys. Then I go home to see panda eyes and red-wine-stained lips!   *Denise*

I'm too old to go clubbing. When my nieces say, 'Come clubbing, Auntie Col,' I think, 'What, bingo?'   *Coleen*

* * *

Dancing queen

Girls and 1970s music are the key elements to a good night out in Jane's world. That's basically it. I've realised that you don't really need men for a good night out, but a lot of women are funny that way. I think there are certain women who are women's women and certain women who prefer men's company.   *Jane*

I like to have a bit of a dance to proper pop music, songs like, 'You To Me Are Everything.' I can't bear monotonous dance music that goes on and on and on. You know – the kind where you go to the toilet and when you come back the same song is playing. It's just awful! *Denise*

After a drink, we all think we're Pan's People! *Jane*

★ ★ ★

Friendship

☆ ☆ ☆

Despite all this talk of 'Frenemies' (friends who are also enemies) the reality is that most of the time our mates are a major source of love and support. Sure, they may drive us mad boasting about their kids' achievements or detailing their romantic woes, but then we know that they'll always be there to pick us up when we're down, or just tell us honestly if our latest bloke's a right plonker. As a group, we've got each other through hard times, and laughed together through the better ones ... Look, you've got us all emotional now!

* * *

The good, the bad and the ugly

I've been in situations with lovely girlfriends who
are seeing people that just aren't right for them.
They know it and you know it and they know that
you know, but you can't say anything. All you can
do is be there for them and wait. *Andrea*

Competitiveness among women can be very destructive.
When people are younger, it's: 'Is your child brighter than
my child? Does your child sleep better than my child?'
So when they get to their fifties, what are they going to
compare? 'Are your wrinkles less visible than mine?' *Lynda*

Maybe women need to have more blokes for friends. Then
they would calm down a little bit and realise that, yes, we
are different, but not necessarily in a bad way. *Andrea*

* * *

Terms of endearment

If you're not careful, you meet these men who do sex and they do handshaking and they don't do anything in between. You've got to teach people to hug.   *Lynda*

It's good to hug. You can always tell when somebody needs a cuddle.   *Zoe*

☆☆ ☆☆ ☆☆ ☆☆

Sometimes a hug says it all. There are times when there's nothing to say except to give somebody a hug.

Lynda

☆☆ ☆☆ ☆☆ ☆☆

I like being called 'hen'. It's a little term of endearment. 'Hello, hen.' It sounds all sort of sweet and clucky.   *Andrea*

I prefer . . . cock. 'You all right, cock?' That's
what they say up North.   *Coleen*

★ ★ ★

Friends and the single girl

When you're single you need to find other single
people to go out with, so I used to find that my girlfriends were getting younger. Some of my girlfriends
were as young as twenty-three, my niece's age!   *Carol*

I just love my gay friends. They make me laugh more than
anybody. I think that gay people have to develop a sense
of humour just to get through, even though homosexual-
ity is much more accepted now. My gay friends are very
loyal, but all my friends are loyal. Perhaps they adore me
in a different way, though. That's not a vanity thing: they
just cherish me a bit more, my gay friends.   *Denise*

It makes sense to hang around with gay men
if you're single, because they're on the same
level as you are. They haven't got kids and as
a result have money to spend.   *Carol*

★ ★ ★

Relationships

☆ ☆ ☆

It's one thing to moon over a man from afar, it's quite another to find yourself washing his socks for the next fifty years. We've all been through far too many ups and downs to believe that once you've got that ring on your finger it's all happy-ever-after. So this is the bit where we take a good hard look at the best bits and the worst bits of relationships. Do opposites really attract? Are men built for monogamy?

And how do you tell if he's Mr Right, or just Mr Alright For Now?

★ ★ ★

True love

I believe in true love. Marriage is a sacred thing and commitment is really impor-tant. People don't think that way anymore, but I'm quite old-fashioned like that.   *Carol*

If you've been damaged before, then you'll always have doubts. The only time you have no doubts is when you don't know what it's like to be let down. You just have to enter a relation-ship with a lot of hope, I think!   *Andrea*

There is a massive difference between fall-ing in love and just loving somebody. I think you get a maximum of eighteen months of that stomach churning stage before you settle into something more secure.   *Denise*

For better, for worse

☆☆ ☆☆ ☆☆ ☆☆

It makes sense that the marriage vows were made when you died aged thirty-five, because no one would have invented it if they'd have known we would live this long!

Denise

☆☆ ☆☆ ☆☆ ☆☆

I was always so focused on a relationship leading to marriage. I went into every relationship thinking, 'This is who I should be 'going for' now.' I was very blinkered and a bit dull. I didn't have much fun. Then I met someone who I knew I didn't want to end up with or marry; I just wanted some fun in my life. It was the best time and it did me good. It made me appreciate the value of a different kind of relationship. *Jane*

If you can get your head round the idea of having a relationship in which he isn't going to be the father of your children and you're not going to marry him, but you have respect for each other and like each other, you can have a fun, sexy time. Then when you do meet somebody that you fall in love with, you can actually tell the difference. *Lynda*

I wish I hadn't suffered quite so much from the Cinderella syndrome when I got married for the first time. I went into it thinking, 'This is it! This is going to be for life!' So I was devastated when I got divorced. I think you should go into a marriage being a bit more realistic. *Jane*

One of my best friends said to me, on the day of her wedding, 'Oh well, if it doesn't work out, we can always get divorced.' I thought, 'What a terrible way to turn up to your wedding.' It makes the whole thing pointless. *Coleen*

I've always said I don't do marriage. I've always maintained that, because I think men find it more desirable if you say that you don't want to get married.   *Lisa*

When you're younger, you have no cynicism. You get married because you're in love and it's all romantic and lovely. But when I was older, getting married seemed like a much more solid, a much more grown-up decision. I wasn't getting married because of, 'Oooh, isn't this romantic and I get to wear a pretty dress for the day!' I was marrying for life, not just for the dress and the party. I think that a lot of girls get so wrapped up in the big day that the anti-climax the next day must be horrendous. They're sitting there, thinking, 'Oh Christ, I'm stuck with him now; this is it!'   *Coleen*

* * *

Cheating hearts

It's in men's psyche to cheat on women. They think about sex every couple of minutes. If you put it in front of them on a plate, they'll eat it, whatever it is, won't they? A woman, on the other hand, will say, 'I might not have that plate. I might have this one, thank you very much, but I will make the choice.' Men just gulp it down in one and it's gone.   *Sherrie*

Statistically, there are as many women having extra-marital affairs as men. I don't think men do it any more than women. There are some women who think about sex every two minutes. Don't tell Tim that I do, because he'll want it!   *Denise*

I've worked out that often men are jealous over you because of what they're doing, or what they know they're capable of doing. So they assume that you're doing the same thing, or are capable of it.   *Coleen*

In a fantasy world, you think, 'Wouldn't it be wonderful if we all were faithful?' But after what happened in my marriage, I would never trust anybody 100 per cent again. I wouldn't go into another relationship with all those wonderful, dreamy expectations. At the end of the day, women don't need sex, but men do; that's always in my mind. *Sherrie*

I don't know any woman who's ever thanked another woman for telling her that her partner's cheating on her. I know quite a few women who have fallen out with women for bringing them that news. *Carol*

I would tell someone if I knew their partner was cheating on them. Absolutely I would. And if they didn't talk to me again, at least they'd know the bloody truth about the person they were living with. I wouldn't do it for myself. I wouldn't do it to keep my friend. I'd do it because I wouldn't want her partner to get away with it. *Sherrie*

Sure, there are probably predatory women out there who deliberately target married men, but I don't think that gives anyone a reason to be suspicious of all women. Women are their own worst enemy a lot of the time. When men have affairs, the wife often blames the other woman, rather than the bloke, when it is the married partner who is completely to blame, in my eyes. He's the one with the responsibility. *Carol*

You don't know what's going on behind closed doors. Some people go out of a marriage to get a bit of love, because they're not getting it within the marriage. It's easy for someone to say, 'Well, just leave!' But sometimes it's difficult to leave, because you've got financial considerations, or kids. So I'm not going to sit and judge anybody for having affairs. It's not as black and white as it sometimes appears. *Jane*

★ ★ ★

Monogamy

I don't want people to think that I'm advocating open marriage, but I think that monogamy is very, very hard. I find it difficult and I think that people who don't find it difficult are usually lying, or nobody ever asks them. It's very easy to say, 'I never would,' if you never get the chance!   *Denise*

Monogamy isn't a natural human trait and it's very difficult for a lot of people, but it's possible. There are people out there who have control and respect for their partner. Not everybody is susceptible to infidelity. I have never been unfaithful to anybody. OK, I have spent most of my life single, so it's not been difficult . . .   *Carol*

Most people, given the temptation and opportunity, would stray.   *Denise*

☆☆ ☆☆ ☆☆ ☆☆

Monogamy is so hard. It's like wearing the same eye shadow all your life. You wouldn't do it!

Denise

☆☆ ☆☆ ☆☆ ☆☆

Relationship MOT

No one is happy 24/7. You are going to hit rocky patches or times when you're sad and think, 'This isn't going to work.' I think the key to it is always working together. It's amazing how much stronger you feel after each stage that you manage to work through together.   *Coleen*

You can tell when you don't make someone happy anymore. It's a gut feeling. Plus, you can tell there's something wrong when you don't feel happy going home.   *Jane*

It's just awful when the laughter goes out of the rela-tionship. Suddenly you're getting on their nerves more, and little things that you've always done are irritat-ing them, or they don't notice you exist.   *Coleen*

What I've learned is that there's a standard that I now have, that I'm secure with, and if people don't reach that standard, there's really not a lot of point in trying to make them come up to it. I won't be horrible to them or anything. I'll just step away.   *Lynda*

☆☆ ☆☆ ☆☆ ☆☆

I wouldn't be in a relationship if it weren't easy and right, because I'm not desperate. While I'm single, I love being single and I would be happy to be single again. So I don't need to be in a relationship.
Carol

☆☆ ☆☆ ☆☆ ☆☆

It's lovely when a relationship is comfortable enough for you to sit in a room together and not speak for an hour or so. That was the good part of my marriage. Yes, I did have a good bit, and that was when we didn't speak!   *Jane*

* * *

Opposites attract?

You have to share the same values with your partner. Many years ago, I was with someone and we had the same values in the beginning. But our values grew apart. He didn't like people really, whereas I'm quite gregarious and love being with people. He wasn't very loyal as a person and I'm a fiercely loyal friend. I'd go on protest marches, because I have a passion about things, and he thought that was really stupid. When you have violent disagreements about values, I don't think there's any point. Eventually it will end.   *Sherrie*

If you suddenly realise that you're not compatible with someone, then maybe you were lying to yourself about being compatible in the first place.   *Carol*

Some people can have radically opposing views, whether it's political or religious differences, but as long as you're still supportive of each other it can work.   *Andrea*

Partners can bring out the best or the worst in you. Paul, my partner, has definitely changed me for the better, because he sets good examples. He's got lovely traits in his personality that I would like to have in my personality. We were watching Beyoncé on the TV the other day; she was singing a song called, 'I don't know why you love me'. It was about someone who's quite a challenging partner. We both looked at each other and knew that only one of us could be singing that song: me!   *Lisa*

☆☆ ☆☆ ☆☆ ☆☆

Letting off steam

Sometimes falling in love isn't the answer to all your problems, is it? Sometimes, your first years together can be the hardest, even when you've met your true love.   *Andrea*

Paul's got some really good argument management practices. If I say, 'Right, I'm leaving you!' he says, 'I'm coming with you!' What do you say to that?   *Lisa*

☆☆ ☆☆ ☆☆ ☆☆

**I don't mind being proved wrong.
I quite like being wrong sometimes. But
it doesn't happen very often!**
Carol

☆☆ ☆☆ ☆☆ ☆☆

I think rowing can be healthy. A friend of mine used to say, 'We never row! We never have a cross moment.' They're divorced now. I think that's because things never got aired. They were both too frightened to have a fight about it, in case the whole thing shattered like glass.   *Andrea*

★ ★ ★

The 'one'

Until I met my husband, I'd always struggled with men who wanted to dominate me. They saw a lively, positive, self-determining woman and they somehow wanted to capture that and contain it. It wasn't until I met Peter that I found somebody whose only ambition was to be my equal. His entire preoccupation was with us sharing everything: the bringing up of children; the earning of a living; and the responsibility for a home. He wanted it all to be entirely fifty-fifty. He is a great feminist, my husband. He was the first man I met who genuinely believed in absolute equality between the sexes. So I married him in a minute! *Lesley*

When Trixie had her heart set on a
man, there was no stopping her.

Despite being divorced and all the hurt that brought, I still believe in a happy-ever-after. The difference now is that I've realised that the only time you achieve perfection is when you stop looking for it. It's quite a profound thing to realise. So I've got to stop wishing everything was perfect and thinking that when everything's perfect, everything will be great, because nothing is ever perfect.   *Andrea*

☆☆ ☆☆ ☆☆ ☆☆

There has to be somebody that you surrender to in life, because you will never truly love anybody if you don't.

Lisa

☆☆ ☆☆ ☆☆ ☆☆

Butterflies in your stomach

I don't believe people when they say, 'I've been married thirty-six years and every time he walks

into the room my tummy turns over.' I think
that's complete and utter rubbish. *Denise*

That initial feeling of butterflies in your stomach when
you know he's about to walk in the room is wonderful, isn't it? But it goes after about a year. It's fabulous when you're thinking, 'God, I'm so nervous, I'm
going to be seeing him tonight!' But then it moves
on to another level, which is equally nice. *Coleen*

There are times in your marriage or long relationship
where you fall back in love with him, when he does something or he sings something, or you see him through other
people's eyes and remember why you fell in love with him.
It's nice when that happens, because you also go through
periods where you could quite happily stab him. *Denise*

How to Keep Romance Alive

☆ ☆ ☆

Alright, so you've picked a good 'un, you've made a home for yourselves, and you've even stopped nagging him about leaving the toilet seat up. What now? Well, contrary to popular opinion, there's more to romance than red roses and it's not just the man's job to keep the spark alive. Even the most blokey bloke secretly wants to know that you still fancy the pants off him . . . even if he does insist on wearing those saggy old Y-fronts. Make a bit of an effort, and who knows what you might get back in return? Oh, and never underestimate the power of a good, old-fashioned snog . . .

★ ★ ★

Making an effort

I don't like vanity, although if you're in a relationship, I don't think it shows a lot of respect for your partner if you let yourself go, even if that sounds shallow. *Carol*

You have to keep excitement going in a marriage. As soon as my ex knew I wouldn't stray, he lost interest. So you have to keep the interest there. *Sherrie*

☆☆ ☆☆ ☆☆ ☆☆

I always try to look marvellous; otherwise it weighs rather heavy if you suddenly make an effort. He might think you're angling for him to have to come and give you one. It's like wearing a flag.

Lynda

☆☆ ☆☆ ☆☆ ☆☆

You don't want to make too much effort when you're first seeing someone, because as time passes it will all taper off and they'll think, 'You don't make an effort anymore!' *Carol*

I like a partner who allows me to feel that I don't have to breathe in the whole time. I can't bear that. In the past, there have been times when I've woken up and thought, 'I must get up, clean my teeth and put my make-up on before I get back into bed!' But those relationships don't last very long. *Jane*

* * *

Snogging

Kissing often gets lost in a long-term relationship, and yet it's so lovely. Amazingly, you get turned on by kissing, even though you think, 'Oh I'm not going to get turned on, because how many times have I done it?' But you do, because something in your brain tells you to. *Lynda*

I think kissing is sexy when he kisses your neck
and then he kisses your ears. If anyone kisses
my ears, my legs go numb.   *Sherrie*

You can't have a marathon snog with someone with
a big moustache and beard, because you don't know
what's in it! There might be things lurking!   *Carol*

I don't like kissing. It's too close; it's too in your face.
Well, I suppose it would be, wouldn't it?   *Sherrie*

I can't bear it if someone kisses my ears. I lean back
to avoid it and then I crick my neck.   *Andrea*

★ ★ ★

True romance

I sleep like a baby, but Tim doesn't, because of my snoring. My
snoring is legendary, but it doesn't bother me at all! It's got

to the point where we go to bed in separate rooms, because Tim is now so obsessed with not getting any sleep because of my snoring that he lies awake waiting for me to start. The moment I make the slightest sound, he yells, 'Oh, I cannot bear it. Get out!' and kicks me out of bed. Meanwhile, he laughs at his own jokes in his sleep and whistles for the dog, so where's the fun in sharing a bed for either of us? Sleeping separately doesn't mean we don't do jiggy-jigs.   *Denise*

It's hard to get everything from one person, but I think it's very important that you absolutely fancy your partner from the get-go, because that diminishes as time goes on.   *Lisa*

Romance can definitely and absolutely last forever. My parents have been married for forty-three years and they still do romantic things. They buy each other little cards and say, 'I love you' all the time. They leave notes for each other, surprise each other and giggle like teenagers. You can hear them in their room, when they're staying with us. They giggle and giggle and giggle, and they're in their sixties.   *Andrea*

'Date Night' had been Raymond's idea. Deborah knew
he was hoping to get lucky but there was no chance.

Sex

☆ ☆ ☆

Well, it's not like sex is *all* we think about (in fact we're quite capable of making a mental shopping list while he's merrily doing his thing. . .) but sooner or later we always seem to end up talking about It. And it's not just a question of how much we're getting, where we're getting it and with whom . . . oh no. In films sex may be all subtle lighting and flattering camera angles, but in real life it's a different thing altogether: good, bad, silly, messy and snuck in while the kids are glued to the telly. So is it overrated? Or are people who say that just not doing it right?

* * *

Alfresco antics

☆☆ ☆☆ ☆☆ ☆☆

I can't be bothered with sex outdoors. If he can't afford a room, I'm not going.

Jane

☆☆ ☆☆ ☆☆ ☆☆

I used to know a couple who really loved having sex outside. After thirty years, he said, 'I want to take you back to where we first had sex.' So they went to the top of this mountain and they made love against a fence. 'My God!' she said. 'That was much better than thirty years ago.' 'Yes, love, but the fence wasn't electrified then!' Boom, boom!   *Denise*

I quite like the idea of sex outdoors, but it scares me too, because I'd be the one either to be caught or to end up in hospital with some horrible sting, having to explain how I got it.   *Coleen*

* * *

Brenda was determined to inject a bit
of spice into the bedroom.

Let's get physical

Sex is my only form of exercise at the moment. It has changed the shape of my legs! They've slimmed down a bit since I met Mark. Everyone gets a bit breathless during sex, don't they? *Carol*

☆☆ ☆☆ ☆☆ ☆☆

I feel fit enough for sex, but I couldn't be doing with the mess! No thank you.

Sherrie

☆☆ ☆☆ ☆☆ ☆☆

A light switch is a wonderful thing. All you have to do to make you body-confident is switch the light off! Never, ever, ever get on top, unless the lights are out. Your face does not look good from that angle. It's not a good look for anybody. *Jane*

I like a bit of buff, but it's not the first thing I go for. I go for the face first. If I find the face attractive, then my eyes move down the body.   *Zoe*

'I lust you,' should be a saying, because a lot of people say, 'I love you,' meaning, 'I lust you.' *Jane*

I have to say that it's been so long that I can't really remember what things look like, so it would be a bit of a jigsaw and I'd have to guess where things go together. The thing is, I'd like somebody with some hard bits, if you know what I mean . . .   *Sherrie*

* * *

Make 'em beg

I do think that sometimes I should put out a bit more when I don't want to. I always know when Tim wants jiggy-jigs and I instantly start complaining about an ache or pain.   *Denise*

If your partner wants sex, you should just let him have it.   *Carol*

☆☆ ☆☆ ☆☆ ☆☆

I've always said, 'Make 'em beg.' After a bit of abstinence, they're very grateful when they do get it!

Jane

☆☆ ☆☆ ☆☆ ☆☆

Luckily, as Tim's got older, his sex drive isn't quite as high. There was a time when I couldn't even bend over and put a dish in the dishwasher without him seeing it as a come-on.   *Denise*

I tell you, when you haven't had it for seven years, once a day ain't enough. Thank God Mark's only twenty-seven!   *Carol*

☆☆ ☆☆ ☆☆ ☆☆

There's an old adage about sex: if people talk about it a lot, it means they're not getting it.

Lynda

☆☆ ☆☆ ☆☆ ☆☆

A lot of people lie about how much sex they have. I remember years ago when I was with one of my exes, a lot of our friends would go on about how they did it five times a night. 'You liars!' I thought. If you did it five times a night, you'd have to sleep all day! It would wear you out! Who does it five times a night? No one!   *Carol*

Some people think that having lots of sex means that it's good sex, but that's not necessarily true at all. It's not about how long it takes or how many partners you have, either. There are women who are able to be completely detached and have sex with a stranger and think it's fabulous, but that doesn't mean that the sex itself is fabulous.   *Lynda*

★ ★ ★

Not tonight, Josephine

Denise has said that she thinks she has a man's attitude to sex. Well, I think I've got an eighty-seven-year-old woman's attitude to sex. I know I've said it before and I'll say it again. I'd rather have a cup of tea. I really would! I think I must be doing it wrong.   *Jane*

☆☆ ☆☆ ☆☆ ☆☆

I think I'm already on the female Viagra! I think Mark's been crushing it up in my cornflakes.

Carol

☆☆ ☆☆ ☆☆ ☆☆

When I was first married, sex was fantastic. And then, oh dear! Anything not to bother . . . I just couldn't be doing with it all. It takes such a long time, doesn't it? You think, 'I could have done this; I could have done that.' I'd do the shopping in my head and have the whole next day lined up. You look at the ceiling and think, 'If I'd only cleaned that cobweb yesterday . . .' *Sherrie*

Sadly, I think there are a lot of women out there who haven't had good sex and so don't actually know what it's like and don't look forward to it. There really are women who lie back and think of England and see it as a chore. If a tablet that enhances sexual pleasure could help women to feel genuine desire and be properly up for it, I'm all for it. *Carol*

I think men should live next door to women. Then you could take them out like ironing boards when you need them! *Jane*

It's difficult to have sex with kids in the house, especially teenagers. As my friend Jackie says, they don't stay in their cots at that age! *Coleen*

* * *

The birds and the bees

When I was young, I learned most of what I knew about sex from my friend at school. She told me everything. She was racy. Then we started babysitting for a couple near where she lived. While they were out, we were very naughty and nosed through their stuff. One day, we came across a stash of rude magazines. After that, we kept going round, offering to babysit, because we couldn't stop looking at the magazines. *Carol*

☆☆ ☆☆ ☆☆ ☆☆

I've learned most of what I know about sex from Denise Welch. She has changed my life.

Jane

☆☆ ☆☆ ☆☆ ☆☆

My first time, we were just getting down to the nitty gritty.
I was there thinking, 'This is it. I'm going to hear the
orchestra playing at any minute.' I'd read Mills & Boon and
so I thought it would be this marvellous experience, albeit
in the back of a camper van in a park. But then I heard all
these people outside and I started thinking, 'They're watching us! There are people outside and they know I'm in here,
doing this!' In fact, they were nicking our petrol.   *Jane*

My first time was behind the church at the local disco
when I was fourteen. My friend had already done it and
everyone in the school was fascinated. They all wanted to
know, 'What happened?' and they wanted to do it as well.

It was like – just get it out of the way! So I went behind the church, did it and probably never spoke to him again. It was 'orrible! It's always horrible the first time, isn't it? *Carol*

* * *

A woman's virtue

Gone are the days when you were told to save yourself for marriage. At the same time, I'm not suggesting that we all go out and are overly promiscuous. But if you truly do find somebody really, really attractive, get on with it, because if it doesn't work, there's no point carrying on. It's no good being in love without the other. *Lynda*

Good sex isn't about technical ability. It's about an emotional bond and that comes with time. When you know someone better, you get a whole load of lovely business going on in your head at the same time. I'd rather be in love than have a drunken fumble. *Lisa*

☆☆ ☆☆ ☆☆ ☆☆

Women sometimes save themselves. 'No, I'm not ready, I'm not ready.' What a waste of time! What if you do finally get there and it is rubbish? You've got to go for it. But not when you first meet them. You've got to have a drink first!

Carol

☆☆ ☆☆ ☆☆ ☆☆

Sex with an emotional connection is always going to be a much better experience. If you love some-body and they're not very good to start with, who's to say that you can't be a great teacher?   *Kate*

* * *

If music be the food of love . . .

I once went out with a guy who was very into building the whole scene: the soft music, the candles. When we first went out, I thought, 'This is lovely!' By the second or third time, I found myself wondering, 'Now what have I got to get tomorrow when I go shopping?' It was taking so long! Ten minutes and I'm bored. So turn the music off, blow out the candles because something's going to catch fire, and let's just get on with it! *Coleen*

I like having music on, if only so the neighbours can't hear, but I don't like it when it's contrived. How can you concentrate on what you're doing if you've got Barry White grunting in the background? That would put me right off my stride! *Carol*

If there's music on in the background, being a singer, all of a sudden I have to burst into the chorus! It's quite off-putting, I must say. Not just for me but for them as well! You say, 'I love this bit,' and he thinks you mean him, when you really mean the upcoming chorus. *Jane*

* * *

Turn-ons/turn-offs

I made a sex tape once, many, many years ago. I watched it back immediately and we looked like two sea lions that needed to be clubbed. It was only two minutes long, but in that two minutes I acted my socks off, let me tell you! I made every possible noise. I'm not joking when I say it was the most hideous thing I've ever watched. I looked like an albino whale. *Coleen*

Erotic fiction works much better for women than visual stimulation. Having said that, I did discover erotic movie videos made for women by women. The difference between those and the ones made by men was amazing. They're so much better. There's nothing less sexy than repetitive close-ups of sex – that's a man's thing. Boring! *Denise*

I think women especially should stop being so insecure about porn. They get very het up about it and see it as an absolute lack of respect. But sometimes men watch it just because they're men and they think about sex a lot. A lot of women say, 'Well if he watches porn it means he doesn't fancy me.' But to me that's a load of rubbish. Porn is there to turn you both on, especially if you're watching it together.   *Coleen*

I remember experiencing a tingle when I first watched *Lady Chatterley's Lover*. There was something about that gamekeeper. It's that whole thing of being taken by somebody who is assertive, not aggressive.   *Denise*

* * *

Kinks and quirks

I once had a boyfriend who was a bit frisky. He said, 'Let's have some mirrors on the ceiling.' I thought, 'That sounds nice. We'll have a bit of that.' But when we had these mirrors put on the ceiling, we could see the bus queue and they could see us!   *Jane*

☆☆ ☆☆ ☆☆ ☆☆

I was staying in a hotel the other day where the headboard of the bed was a mirror. How hideous is that? I said to Ray, 'The only thing I'm going to watch is me having a headache. It ain't happening unless we put gaffer tape over it.'

Coleen

☆☆ ☆☆ ☆☆ ☆☆

A couple of Christmases ago, Ed bought black satin sheets to spice things up. I thought, 'This is great!' I bought some lovely silk pyjamas to go with them. But then I got in one side and slid right out the other! I was hanging on for grim death. Now I know what those handles are for on the sides of the mattress! *Jane*

Like most men, Ray loves the idea of me dressing up. I initially bought a nurse's outfit for a laugh. Then I mentioned it on *Loose Women*, and I've since had three outfits sent to me . . . for free! Now I've got a nurse's outfit and a policewoman's uniform and a naughty housewife costume – I am a naughty housewife, anyway, because I don't clean the house enough! *Coleen*

I can't bear the idea of stripograms. I don't think there is anything sexy about a bloke taking his clothes off in a room full of people and being pointed at and humiliated. *Lisa*

☆☆ ☆☆ ☆☆ ☆☆

I'd prefer a pedicure to a stripper.
Andrea

☆☆ ☆☆ ☆☆ ☆☆

I come from a time and a background where even to say the word 'vibrator' would make you feel quite sick. You couldn't even say it, let alone think that somebody actually used one. *Sherrie*

Phone sex seems a bit silly to me. What's the point? I can't be arsed. *Carol*

I recommended a series of books to Jane about women's sexual fantasies. Let's just say that it's helped her develop her phone relationship with Ed!   *Denise*

I'll tell you something: the phone bill's tripled.   *Jane*

★ ★ ★

Quality quickies

I can't do with quickies, forget it! You know, if you're not going to make the effort, then don't call me!   *Jane*

When you've got young kids, it's often a quickie. I've said it before and I'll say it again: it just depends how long an episode of *Peppa Pig* it is. If it's on satellite, they'll sometimes show three episodes in a row, one after another, so you get about twenty minutes!   *Andrea*

I've got a switch-off mode when my daughter is around. I've got used to switching from sexy partner mode into mother mode and never the twain shall meet! *Lisa*

Tantric sex takes a very long time. Some people don't want it to be long and drawn out; they just want to get on with it and get to sleep. *Jane*

Anticipation is very important, but I don't want all that contrived rose petals and candles and music. So I just delay it by saying, 'Right, I'll just go and put some washing on.' Or, 'I'm just going to empty that cupboard.' Then he'll send me a text message from downstairs, saying, 'Get down here!' By that time, he's in a right old frenzy. *Carol*

★ ★ ★

The good sex guide

☆☆ ☆☆ ☆☆ ☆☆

Good sex is a bit like a fillet steak. You get fed up with it if you have it every night and sometimes you just fancy a burger!

Jane

☆☆ ☆☆ ☆☆ ☆☆

I feel very sorry for young men these days. I think it's up to young women to use their emotional intelligence to make young men feel better about themselves. Girls should tell them what's good, what's comfortable and what's rewarding. Maybe that's how emotional intelligence really works: you make him feel good about himself, and you'll get a lot more back from the boys.   *Lynda*

There are so many old blokes about who haven't got a clue what they're doing, because a load of women have always said, 'Oh you're brilliant!' when they're not. We tiptoe around the male ego too much. Women are their own worst enemy when it comes to things like that. They shouldn't do it.   *Carol*

They say that when you're young you should meet an older man who will teach you things, and then you will go on to understand. Well, I never had any of that. I just had fumbling innocents.   *Sherrie*

If a woman told me, 'My husband is boring in bed,' I'd say back to her, 'Are you sure it's not you who's boring?'   *Lynda*

There is nothing like that first knicker-ripping stage of a relationship, but there is also something nice about long-term sex. You can take your time, your partner knows what buttons to press and you're not having to put on a performance.   *Denise*

☆☆ ☆☆ ☆☆ ☆☆

Sex is very much trial and error. What you find pleasurable someone else might not, so you need to learn about each other and be able to laugh when it all goes tits up.

Coleen

☆☆ ☆☆ ☆☆ ☆☆

Male libido

It always amazes me when people say, 'I don't mind him when he's drunk, because he doesn't want sex and falls asleep.' My husband's the opposite! It doesn't matter what time he has come in; it could be four or five in the morning and he might be bladdered, but the one thing he'll want is sex.

I always know, because he starts stroking my arm. Oh God, please! If I've been out with him, it's fair enough, but if I've been in bed for the last four hours and I've got to do the school run, it's just annoying. Either you've got to lie there and pretend to be asleep, or you just let him and it goes on and on and on – because he's so drunk that nothing's happening – while you're lying there, thinking, 'Please hurry up and get it over with!' *Coleen*

A two-hour, child-free gap means different things to men and women. He sees it as an opportunity for sex, while the woman is thinking, 'How much housework can I get done before the baby wakes up?' *Denise*

Just the other morning, Ray turned into me and we were spooning! Unheard of! Anyway, the spooning didn't last for long. Afterwards, two minutes later, I said to him, 'Raymondo, is there any chance that one time we could have a little cuddle in bed and a little spoon that doesn't lead to *that*.' He said, 'No.'
A man after my own heart; I love him! *Coleen*

The thing about husbands or partners giving you a massage is that you end up saying, 'My inner thigh wasn't the place that I wanted massaging.' There's always that tendency and you think, Oh, not jiggy-jigs! I just want to go to sleep!'   *Denise*

* * *

Living without it?

I actually found that my life was much less complicated without sex, because it tends to cloud your thoughts and your judgement. You become, not obsessed . . . but distracted. Now I am sexually active again, I can't believe I went seven years without it, but what you don't have, you don't miss. If a woman wants to have sex, it's very easy to get someone to do it with her. I was quite happy not to do it.   *Carol*

If I had to choose between not having sex again and not having a massage again, I'd be really torn. Massage is my most favourite thing in the entire world. I could be massaged 24/7, all year round, and never get tired of it. Not sure if I feel quite the same about sex!   *Denise*

☆☆ ☆☆ ☆☆ ☆☆

I like sex; I just don't do it anymore!
Sherrie

☆☆ ☆☆ ☆☆ ☆☆

Sex is vastly overrated.   *Jane*

Moving Forward

☆ ☆ ☆

After all that smut and nonsense it's time to get a bit more serious. When you're in a relationship and it's good, the whole world looks rosy. But we all know people (ourselves included) who've hung onto a bad relationship because they were too scared to face the reality: that it was time to move on. The good thing about us girls is that we can be brutally honest with each other and say, 'You're too good for that.' Sometimes life feels like it's crashing down around you, but we've all been through dark times and managed to come out laughing . . . eventually!

* * *

Knowing when to say goodbye

I don't do 'closure'. I don't need it.   *Carol*

I need to know everything's done, dusted and sorted emotionally before I move on. I go back to things years later because they're haunting me. One particular situation I remember: I had a relationship with somebody I shouldn't have had a relationship with. When I got married, I sat there and thought, 'That was really wrong.' So I phoned him up and said, 'I'm really sorry for doing what I did and ruining your life.' That was closure for me. Purely selfish, I know, but I felt better.   *Zoe*

Why stay with someone who makes you really unhappy, especially if you have the same effect on them? Life is too short to be a martyr. It's such a short time that we've got on this planet and it's up to you what you do.   *Jane*

☆☆ ☆☆ ☆☆ ☆☆

If you're in love with someone who doesn't want you and you've got to get over it, you should leave. Get out; big break; separation. If somebody doesn't want me, I'm not going to hang around and waste my love.

Lynda

☆☆ ☆☆ ☆☆ ☆☆

If it's not going to work, it's not going to work. If it's gone, it's gone. You can't make someone love you. Fortunately, there are lots of other people out there who will love you. 'Plenty more fish in't sea,' as my gran used to say. It used to annoy me when I was younger, but it's a phrase I use all the time now! *Jane*

* * *

Breaking up is hard to do

Breaking up is definitely like a bereavement. You're mourning what could have been, as well as what you had at the beginning. You need time to grieve, even if you're the one who left, not the one who has been left. A lot of people make the mistake of thinking that it's all right for the one who left. It's really not. *Andrea*

You can't rush something like that. If you want to grieve, grieve as much as you want. If you don't want to go out, don't go out. It's your body dealing with it and your mind getting through it. It can take some people six months; it can take some people six years; and it did take me an awful long time. *Jane*

I always say to people when their relationship ends, 'Don't think you've got to go and find somebody else.' I'm suspicious of people who go through break-ups and waltz straight into the next relationship. Still, I'm a bit more that way than some people are. I tend to dust myself down and start all over again. The trouble with me is that I'm so busy trying to start again and forget it that I don't learn any lessons from it. You also need to look at the mistakes you've made. You can't possibly have been with someone for sixteen or twenty years and just turn it all off. It's got to work its way through. Everybody should be on their own for a bit, really on their own. Especially men, because they're very bad at it. I learned to be confident when I was on my own and it's the only way to understand what makes you tick. *Lynda*

There's not a lot of point in going through bad experiences if you don't learn from them, is there? *Andrea*

★ ★ ★

Alone, not lonely

Bitterness and regret are very unattractive. During the ten years I was on my own, I nearly went down the cracks. All that sitting in the kitchen with friends and copious bottles of wine, getting fatter and more bitter.   *Lynda*

You have to be on your own to find your true self. Then you can meet the right guy. I'd had boyfriends continuously since I was fourteen when I found myself on my own at thirty-nine, for nine months, no sex, no nothing. After a while, I began to get the hang of it. I thought, 'I can do this! I can be independent; I can be strong; I can do without a man.' Of course, then I met Peter. I didn't need anyone, I wasn't bothered, and he came through the door. It's because I'd found myself and I knew who I was.   *Lesley*

Independence can imprison you. There's this place called 'the waiting room', where you go and shut the door when you're on your own too long. Carol was in the waiting room for seven years, but she happened to open the door to get the milk and Mark popped in. You have to get out of the waiting room. I've put a lock on my door, but fortunately I've found my buzzer.   *Sherrie*

We don't need men like we used to. In my mum's day and back into my gran's day, the only time you could really live alone was when you were widowed. Women in those days couldn't afford to leave the house, because they had nowhere to go and they had no jobs; they were kept. Whereas now women are able to be career women, they can survive on their own.   *Jane*

☆☆ ☆☆ ☆☆ ☆☆

A man can't live without a woman, but women are beginning to be able to live without men.

Sherrie

☆☆ ☆☆ ☆☆ ☆☆

Getting over it

I like a wallow. One particular break-up was like a bereavement for me; it took me a long time to get over it. I was devastated; it was a massive thing. So I took the bottle of vodka and retired to the bathroom, many a night! And the pain went. It was marvellous. I'm not very good at crying in public, so I like to hole myself away and have a good cry. I spent about nine months drinking vodka in the bathroom! *Jane*

The tendency to wallow is a bit irritating, I find. We've all got friends who've done that. After a while you think, 'Shut up!' After a while, you need to move on. *Lynda*

Obviously it's very hurtful when you find out that your partner's been unfaithful. It really knocks your confidence. Still, it might be worthwhile to accept that maybe you could have done some things better, but didn't. But don't blame yourself! After that, just get happy, because they hate it when you get happy; they bloody hate it when you get over them! *Coleen*

I know it sounds trite, but to see people struggling with illness or disability really puts things in perspective. You think to yourself, 'I'd better shut up.' *Lynda*

I think reinventing yourself is a very important thing. That's why I move house a lot. When I broke up with my ex, I had to turn over so many blooming leaves that I had a whole tree of them going over. I don't even know my address anymore, really. *Sherrie*

How to be Happy

☆ ☆ ☆

Seems like these days everybody is looking for the same elusive thing: happiness. Whether you find it in a church, at a yoga class or down your local pub (Carol, we're with you on that one!) you owe it to yourself to make the most out of life. In this section we'll let you into our little secrets: how to keep smiling when it's raining outside, you're running late and you've just laddered your last pair of tights. Basically, it all comes down to wanting what you've got, not getting what you want ... although that can be nice too!

★ ★ ★

My mantra

I don't want to know what's round the corner.
I just want to live for today. *Jane*

Now that the break-up of my marriage and all those horrible times are behind me, I try to wake up every morning
and smile and say thank you. I've got a lot to say thank
you for, especially my daughter and my grandson, and I
always think that if you can just smile first thing in the
morning, then the rest of the day will be OK. *Sherrie*

You can look like a supermodel, but ultimately it
comes down to how happy you are as a person,
who you're with and if they love you for you
and not just something to look at. *Coleen*

It's naff and it's 70s but I've always lived by the
mantra, 'Feel the fear and do it anyway.' Also, 'If
it feels right, it is right, and if it feels wrong, it is

wrong.' It's really straightforward and I always use it. It's about trusting your instincts.   *Andrea*

☆☆ ☆☆ ☆☆ ☆☆

How important is it to get in touch with your spiritual side? Depends if you need it or not. I don't need it. I worship at the altar of the Rose and Crown.
Carol

☆☆ ☆☆ ☆☆ ☆☆

Positive attitude

I truly believe that if you try to make a plan and achieve certain goals, good things are more likely to happen to you.   *Lynda*

☆☆ ☆☆ ☆☆ ☆☆

I think I'm happy because I don't have any
expectations. I think it's a good thing, because
I'm never disappointed. If you don't expect
too much, then everything is great. If I get
up in the morning and think, 'It's going to be
a fantastic day,' and it's not, I'm going to be
upset. But if I get up without that expectation,
then it's all great.

Carol

☆☆ ☆☆ ☆☆ ☆☆

Ageing

☆ ☆ ☆

Now, if the world was a fair place then society at large (and men, in particular) would value mature women for their wit, wisdom and sexual allure. Beauty would ripen like a fine wine, not go off like a pint of semi-skimmed. Sadly we're stuck in the real world of cellulite, wrinkles and saggy bosoms, and the men our age all seem to be getting midlife crises and lusting after leggy twenty-somethings. But why should they have all the fun? After all, you're only as old as the man you're feeling (boom boom!) and, besides, there are plenty of ways to grow old disgracefully . . .

★ ★ ★

Looking on the bright side

☆☆ ☆☆ ☆☆ ☆☆

I'm actually quite looking forward to the menopause, because for the first time I'll be warm.

Jane

☆☆ ☆☆ ☆☆ ☆☆

You have to face your fears as you get older. I think you should do more and be less fearful when you're faced by mortality. Think to yourself: 'Hey, you're dead a long time, so why not do it?' *Sherrie*

I care a lot less as I get older. I think, 'You know what? This is me!' Whatever you see in the mirror, if you're happy inside, you exude that happiness and that's very attractive. *Coleen*

Since I hit the big 5-0, I don't care as much anymore. I'm not bothered about being unfavourably compared with other people. I feel happier in my own skin than I have done before. *Denise*

* * *

Staying young

It's good to do things that scare you, because you can be too safe as you get older. I don't even really like driving up the motorway anymore, yet when I was seventeen, I'd get in my car and drive up to Birmingham to go to a disco. *Carol*

The older you get and the more children you have, the more fearful you become. You're afraid of things that you wouldn't have even considered before. I used to be scared to death of spiders, but I don't care about spiders now, I care about flying, about dying, about mortality, because I've got kids. *Lesley*

When you're younger, you don't believe in failure. You just don't see it.   *Lynda*

☆☆ ☆☆ ☆☆ ☆☆

My tip for looking good over forty? The best thing you can do is get a young man.

Carol

☆☆ ☆☆ ☆☆ ☆☆

Older men vs younger men

Men seem to be catching on and catching up. There are wonderful older men – and younger men, actually; look at Carol! – who have great respect for older women and see us in a very different way. You meet men who want to match you and understand how you've come to be so strong. A lot of men don't want women who are needy and weak, especially the kind of men that we'd be attracted to.   *Lesley*

Men get away with ageing so much more easily than women. They don't get judged so much. Fortunately, I like a rugged, kicked-in-looking face on a man, which my husband is not particularly happy about me saying! *Coleen*

I've heard from young men who say that young women don't want to hang out in a hotel room making passionate love all day. Can you believe it? Apparently, young women don't want to get messy. It's quite the opposite with older women, which is probably why younger men find them so attractive. 'Stay here, young man! You're not going anywhere . . .' *Lynda*

Every woman should have a younger man at some point in her life. *Jane*

Younger man–older woman is the right way round, because we last longer. *Lynda*

Men my age have all turned into strange people who want twenty-year-old flesh. They don't want a woman my age. So you have to go for slightly younger men who haven't reached that weird life crisis stage yet.   *Sherrie*

Being with a younger man is great as long as you don't fall in love, because obviously that would end in tears, at some point. It's in your control to turn this young man into the perfect lover and future husband for someone else.   *Lynda*

I appreciate younger men and I appreciate it if a younger man ever fancies me, but as far as a long-term relationship goes, I'm not into younger men. Enrique Iglesias is just beautiful and sooo gorgeous. I couldn't take my eyes off him when he came on the show. But if I went out with him, it would make me feel old.   *Coleen*

☆☆ ☆☆ ☆☆ ☆☆

Younger men should be prescribed on the NHS!

Jane

☆☆ ☆☆ ☆☆ ☆☆

Looking in the mirror

There's so much pressure on women to look
young, and fighting it is really hard. It really
gets me down, but I am fighting it. *Carol*

Getting old is very hard. You look in the mirror and think,
'Who's that? Where's the other woman who used to look
back at me?' You feel the same, but she's not there. *Sherrie*

I had my eyes done because I looked tired
all the time. I was up half the night worrying about my wrinkles, that's why! *Jane*

You know when you're in the bathroom sometimes
and you turn round and catch that look? What is all
that hanging around? You stuff it in your knickers and
try and hold it in, but it doesn't stay there. *Sherrie*

* * *

Love your wrinkles

There's no point in doing anything about my wrinkles, because everyone knows this is what I look like now. Anyway, if I start having things done, I'll just end up looking like everybody else.   *Carol*

☆☆ ☆☆ ☆☆ ☆☆

I like seeing people age. I like seeing life on people's faces. I think I've earned my lines. They really don't bother me.

Coleen

☆☆ ☆☆ ☆☆ ☆☆

I don't mind my wrinkles. Still, I'll go on saving up for a bit more surgery – what the heck!   *Jane*

If you have a wrinkle you don't like, do something about it. Wrinkles are interesting things. I really like some of my wrinkles. I'm happy to own the wrinkles that represent the laughter that's been in my life. I'm also quite fond of wrinkles that represent curiosity in my life. And there aren't that many wrinkles that represent sadness, because I've done something about those! I want my face to represent the person I am, and there is nothing sad about me.   *Lesley*

* * *

Mutton dressed as lamb

I don't feel old yet, but I'm quite conscious of mutton dressed as lamb and I'm perfectly aware that there are parts of my body that are best left covered up, unless I can lie down, breathe in and put my hands above my head!   *Lynda*

When you get older you have to make a choice: it's either your face or your body. If you want your face to stay not too bad, it has to be at the expense of the waist and the tummy, I'm afraid. If you want to stick to a size eight, your face will go. So, do you want a very thin gaunt face or do you want a bit of weight on it?   *Sherrie*

I think that each stage in your life has clothing that is appropriate for it or that you feel comfortable in. That doesn't mean it won't be glamorous, sexy or interesting as you get older. On the contrary, the older I get the more confident I feel to explore all the things that are possible. There are some things that I would just feel silly in now, but I would have felt silly in other things when I was younger. You've got to wear what expresses who you are at that particular moment in your life.   *Lesley*

★ ★ ★

Fabulous at fifty

When you're in your twenties, you think you're going to be like that for ever. You can't imagine being forty or forty-five; it just seems so ridiculous. It's tantamount to being dead. *Carol*

Fifty used to be an over-the-hill age, but thankfully it's very different now. *Denise*

Fifty is an amazing age for a woman. I've felt extremely free in my fifties. It's as if everything is a bonus. Ours is almost the first generation where the fifties have been such a liberating time. Jackie Collins and all those wonderful women who used to be on *Dallas* and *Dynasty* were probably the founding mothers of the fabulous fifties club and now women in society in general are a part of it. Now we can be who we want to be: sexy, glamorous, youthful and fit. We're powerful and autonomous; we're self-sufficient. *Lesley*

☆☆ ☆☆ ☆☆ ☆☆

It can be difficult if you've never had a problem getting boys and suddenly the attention isn't there. I thought, 'God it's happened!' But then suddenly, at fifty-one, I find it's gone the other way. I'm not going to do anything about it, but it's very nice.

Denise

☆☆ ☆☆ ☆☆ ☆☆

Grooming and Self-Image

☆ ☆ ☆

Alright, we admit it. There are some days when we look in the mirror and all we see are wrinkles and tired eyes, and not the gorgeous, feisty, fun-filled women looking back at us. So we flash our cash on a load of beauty products because, like the ads say, *we're worth it*, but what have we got to show in return? Do any of these miracle products actually – whisper it – work? Well, whether you're a tanorexic or a beauty parlour phobic you've probably got a fair bit to say on the subject. And so, of course, have we!

* * *

Shelby has applied to *Ten Years Younger* fourteen times now.

Mirror, mirror

☆☆ ☆☆ ☆☆ ☆☆

My motto is: 'Only dull people look good in the morning.'

Denise

☆☆ ☆☆ ☆☆ ☆☆

Most women have dimples on the backs of their
legs in the wrong light. You can't let it get you
down. What can you do about it?   *Carol*

When did I look my finest? It's right now. I'm loving it.   *Jane*

I've never been pretty. I was told I would never work
until I was forty. (Proved them wrong!) Now I'm happy.
I go with the flow. I think I've got a man because I
go in and give it some welly. It's a case of, 'Take me
or leave me.' (I also tell very good jokes.)   *Lynda*

My face doesn't match my personality, because I have a naturally miserable looking face, even though I'm happier now than perhaps I've ever been. I make an effort to smile, but I'm not going to have my face stitched up like the Joker.   *Carol*

If you don't like how your boobs look when you're naked, don't buy a full-length mirror. If it's a half mirror, I can't see my boobs!   *Coleen*

* * *

Confidence tricks

I don't know what makes a woman sexy. It's all down to the person who finds her sexy. Before I met my fiancé, I didn't feel sexy at all. If anybody said they fancied me, I'd think, 'Don't be ridiculous, you're lying.' Now, because he really does find me sexy, I think, 'Maybe I am a bit sexy sometimes!' It's strange, isn't it?   *Carol*

☆☆ ☆☆ ☆☆ ☆☆

Now I've got my confidence, I just love life.
It's grand. I love myself so much that if
I were chocolate, I'd eat myself!

Jane

☆☆ ☆☆ ☆☆ ☆☆

If I'm trying to impress people, I just think, 'This is
me. If you're not impressed, that's tough!'   *Carol*

★ ★ ★

Inner beauty

I think power is more attractive than beauty sometimes.
That's why politicians still manage to pull!   *Jane*

You can have a woman with the most beautiful face and
body in the world, but if she hasn't got anything to say,

it's boring. Once you've initially thought, 'Wow!' unless the whole package is there, it's very dull.   *Coleen*

If I don't put my face on first thing in the morning, I literally scare children!   *Jane*

People make this terrible mistake of thinking you can hide your lines. Well, you can't.   *Lynda*

At the risk of looking like Joan Crawford in *Mommie Dearest*, I've had my eyebrows tattooed. I over-plucked mine when I was eleven, back in the days when you plucked them all out, and they've never grown back. Now I just keep them smooth with a bit of Vaseline every day!   *Denise*

★ ★ ★

High-maintenance?

I can honestly say that my skin is no better when I'm using expensive potions and lotions, cleansing, toning and moisturising, than when I fall asleep in my make-up, which I regularly do. I'm openly admitting that I'm a complete slut at night-time! I'm often so tired that I'll fall asleep on the settee and stagger up to bed later.   *Denise*

I was fake-tanned for the Baftas, which was horrible. You have to stand up in a pair of paper knickers while this complete stranger looks at you stark naked, saying, 'OK, arms up for me,' and 'Turn around.' It's just so undignified and you suddenly start smelling like an old carrot. It may look nice, but it's only good as long as nobody comes anywhere near you. And it absolutely annihilated my white bed linen. My pillow had a little brown head imprint in the middle, showing where my face had been during the night.   *Lisa*

☆☆ ☆☆ ☆☆ ☆☆

Tanned women always say they love my pale complexion. In fact, they love it so much that they plaster themselves in fake tan.

Coleen

☆☆ ☆☆ ☆☆ ☆☆

Brown flesh is not as bad as really pale and pasty, white mashed potato flesh. It looks much better. Some of those girls you see out falling down in the street on the news, they need to put a bit of fake tan on, because their legs look like stuffing.   *Carol*

* * *

'Me' time

I get very selfish with my 'me' time. I like to have half an hour every night to watch a serial killer documentary and if I don't have it, I get very angry!   *Denise*

The bathroom is the only place in the house where I
can lock the door and get a bit of peace without anyone
wondering why. I can stay in the bath for four hours.   *Lisa*

☆☆ ☆☆ ☆☆ ☆☆

A lot of pampering is a good thing.
Lynda

☆☆ ☆☆ ☆☆ ☆☆

I have to have candles lit all the time – otherwise my brain addles, because I have an insane life.
I find them very soothing and calming.   *Sherrie*

My advice to any busy working mum would be to try and
take an hour a day, or an hour every couple of days, to
think about yourself or do something for yourself. But I
know how hard it is. You just don't do it, do you?   *Coleen*

★ ★ ★

Jill couldn't believe that all that pain had
left her with one tiny hair-free patch.

Miracle cream

I'm what you might call a moisturiser slut. Day
cream, night cream: I'll try anything.   *Andrea*

It's sad that women buy into the idea that if you use
this cream, you're going to look like Andie MacDowell
or whoever's doing the commercial. It's hard not to
think that women are a bit stupid sometimes.   *Carol*

☆☆ ☆☆ ☆☆ ☆☆

Fifty quid for a pot of face cream? You are having a laugh. I'd want you to give me a face-lift for fifty quid!

Coleen

☆☆ ☆☆ ☆☆ ☆☆

Here come the girls!

Cosmetic Surgery

☆ ☆ ☆

When women start discussing plastic surgery the knives really start coming out. At one end of the scale are people who think that it's sad, vain and dangerous, while at the other end are people who celebrate it as safe, useful and empowering. So does Mother Nature really know best, or could she use a helping hand? Often, people who might have rejected it in their twenties and thirties start to come round to the idea of a bit of Botox, or a subtle nip and tuck to keep them looking youthful. You'll find the full spectrum of opinion among us Loose Women and, as usual, we're prepared to argue the toss!

* * *

Botox, baby

The thing about the Botox look is that everybody looks like they're rabbits caught in the headlights. It's bad enough on women, but if the men are going to do it too, we all might as well be in a sci-fi film. *Lynda*

☆☆ ☆☆ ☆☆ ☆☆

Botox? Yes, of course I have Botox. Even my cat has Botox!

Lesley

☆☆ ☆☆ ☆☆ ☆☆

Almost everybody I know has had fillers and they're all walking around with their faces puffed out. I can't bear it. If I had fillers, I would look like a fat chipmunk. Fillers give you big baby faces. You don't have any lines, but you've got this big baby face. I would hate that. *Sherrie*

★ ★ ★

Under the knife

I no longer spend money on creams or potions. I'd rather save it for surgery and go straight for the kill!   *Denise*

☆☆ ☆☆ ☆☆ ☆☆

If you have cosmetic surgery, it should be for the right reasons, not because of some man or to escape heartache.

Sherrie

☆☆ ☆☆ ☆☆ ☆☆

In my mum's day, nobody had cosmetic surgery and you just accepted people for what they were. You'd say, 'She doesn't look great for her age,' or, 'God, she looks good for eighty-five!' Now you say, 'She looks good. What is she, about forty?' And someone replies, 'No she's eighty-five.'   *Coleen*

I say yes to cosmetic surgery if it works for you. It's all about how you feel, not whether everybody else says, 'Oh my God, that's fantastic!' If you look in the mirror and you're happy with what you see, then it has worked. *Jane*

You have to wonder what's going on in the heads of people who have masses of plastic surgery. Are they doing it because the man in their life has a) told them to, or b) made them feel they should have it done? Invariably he leaves them for the younger model anyway. So they're on a hiding to nothing. *Lynda*

I would never tell someone not to have a facelift and I wouldn't judge him or her. It's your face and your body, so do what you like. *Carol*

My biggest fear would be to look in the mirror and not to recognise myself. *Lesley*

★ ★ ★

Celebrity surgery

I hate it when people don't admit they've had cosmetic surgery! Or if they claim their shape is all down to genes or luck. Jane Fonda went on about her healthy lifestyle while she was secretly suffering from bulimia.   *Lynda*

In America they can take your face off, stretch it and put it back. If I had that done, I'd want Julia Roberts' face instead of my old face back, thank you very much!   *Sherrie*

It's just not acceptable to look your age anymore. It's hard, but you just have to fight it. You have to think about it a lot and accept that this is what happens to everybody. You can have a load of work done, but eventually you're going to look old; it's going to happen whatever you do. Either that or you're going to end up looking like Joan Rivers.   *Carol*

The World of Showbiz

☆ ☆ ☆

It's not all glitz and glam, you know! Being in the public eye means having your love-life and your cellulite scrutinised in the magazines and newspapers when you least expect it. No one wants to see a big red circle drawn around their wobbly bits. Where's airbrushing when you need it? But we can't complain really, since there's so much fabulous stuff about being on *Loose Women*. One of the best *best* things is that we actually get to touch (and even fondle a bit) some of our all-time top celebrity crushes. It's a tough job, we know, but someone's got to do it . . .

★ ★ ★

Oh b****r – she'd only popped out for some milk.

Media circus

I'm a real punter when it comes to reading the papers. I'm like, 'Can you believe what so-and-so did?' and then it turns out to be totally untrue. I still love reading all the gossip, though, even about myself. I'll read something and think, 'Really? I didn't know I did that!' I don't mind. It just makes me laugh.   *Coleen*

Slowly it's beginning to dawn on the public that when you pick up a magazine and you see somebody on the front cover with not a line on their face, not a pimple, not an eyelash out of place, then maybe, maybe, the photograph has been airbrushed. Now, there's nothing wrong with good lighting, there's nothing wrong with enhancing what you've got, but it's terrible trying to con young women by airbrushing models and taking out all the fat.   *Lynda*

☆☆ ☆☆ ☆☆ ☆☆

The other day, I saw a woman I know on a magazine cover. She's forty-five and she looked ten. I thought, 'How sad,' because you can't see who she is.

Sherrie

☆☆ ☆☆ ☆☆ ☆☆

The show must go on

When you grow up in show business – and by that I mean live performing – it really is a case of 'the show must go on'. In TV, on the other hand, some-one only needs to have a slight headache to say, 'I must have the day off!' You think, 'Oh shut up!'   *Coleen*

I go on, no matter what's wrong with me. You'd really have to be dead or dying to be allowed off a performance. My worst ever experience was when I had food poisoning during a production of the musical *Salad Days*. I was sick and had diarrhoea in a bucket at the side of the stage in between scenes! That was a Saturday night in Birmingham never to be forgotten!   *Lynda*

★ ★ ★

Celebrity crushes

What do people find attractive about Russell Brand? I don't get it.   *Jane*

I think Simon Cowell is absolutely gorgeous. It's not even a looks thing for me. Perhaps it's because he's so good at what he does. He's got a fantastic brain, he's very powerful, which I think is very attractive, and I love the fact that he obviously loves his mum. I met him once and he was with his mum. You got the impression that he would do anything she asked. I love that.   *Lisa*

☆☆ ☆☆ ☆☆ ☆☆

From a fancying point of view, Simon Cowell is too smooth. I like them a bit rough around the edges. Do you know what I mean? I like a builder!

Denise

☆☆ ☆☆ ☆☆ ☆☆

Do you not think that if Simon Cowell were chocolate, he'd eat himself? *Jane*

Cliff Richard is a lot of things – he's brilliant, he's talented, he's still around and he looks fantastic – but he's not a sex symbol. David Beckham is a sex symbol, because he's sexy looking. Sex symbols can grow out of their symbolism! Give it twenty years and Brad Pitt won't be a sex symbol, he'll just be an old man.   *Carol*
I think Ronaldo's mum would like me as a daughter-in-law. What have I got to offer? We haven't got time to list everything. The first thing I'd do is go home and hide all the wax, so he looked a bit more like a bloke. I'd take away all the

mirrors. He's gorgeous to look at, but he's too perfect. He needs a bit of roughing up and I'm the girl to do it.   *Coleen*

* * *

Twentieth-century icons

Madonna had nothing to do with my sexual liberation, which she may have done for others. I was sexually liberated way before that madam came along and started doing it.   *Denise*

Why is everybody so thin? What happened to proper curves? I like Sophia Loren, because that woman eats pasta. She's class, but she has a good meal. That's all I'm asking for.   *Jane*
My ideal image of myself would be Katherine Hepburn, who was five-foot-eleven, and she wore those wonderful baggy trousers with pleats. I love that look, but then I realise that I'm five-foot-four and not very thin!   *Lynda*

If a woman holds herself well and moves well and has a confidence about her body, it's very sexy, whoever she is. Helen Mirren is exactly that, for me. She has that fantastic way of standing. She's in command, in control. She's going to give you a good time.   *Lesley*

I want everything to be like a film and I get so frustrated when it isn't. I spend my life saying to Ray, 'You're so not Cary Grant!' I'd love our life to be like Cary Grant's and Doris Day's in all of those films.
I say to Ray, 'Cary Grant wouldn't say that.'
'That's because he's a knob,' he says. But Cary Grant wouldn't even know the word 'knob'!   *Coleen*

The Mysteries of Men

☆ ☆ ☆

Growing up, boys seemed like creatures from another planet, with their sprouting facial hair, dubious personal hygiene and bulging underpants. To be honest, not that much has changed. They say men are from Mars and, if that's the case, you can bet that planet is clogged up with dirty old socks and soggy towels. No wonder they came down to Earth – they needed someone to clean up after them! Another theory is that men are like dogs, and all they need is a little training. Read on for some tried-and-tested tips on how to house-train your fella. Heel, boy!

★ ★ ★

What do men actually get up to in sheds?

Rules of attraction

☆☆ ☆☆ ☆☆ ☆☆

I only smoulder with somebody I don't think I'm going to cop off with, because if I really fancy someone, I can't even speak to them!

Jane

☆☆ ☆☆ ☆☆ ☆☆

I once said to a bloke, 'To be honest, I really like you, but I just don't fancy you.' He said, 'Well, that's quite good, because I don't really fancy you, either.' Suddenly, I really fancied him! I sat there saying, 'No, you *do* really fancy me.'   *Coleen*

When you're a teenager, you can fall madly, madly in love and you're so in love. Then you meet the next day and he's got a spot. 'Eurgh!!!' Suddenly it's all off.   *Lynda*

I quite like an accent. I like a guttural sound, but
I like it very deep. I mean the voice, of course!
You dirty lot! I like a deep voice.   *Jane*

★ ★ ★

The chase

I don't see the point in chasing a man. If he's
not interested, he's not interested.   *Lynda*

They come up with all these terms like 'phone
phobia', but if he doesn't call, he's just not into
you! Move on. Get another one.   *Carol*

With a man, it's a big step to say 'I love you' – and
then God forbid if they don't love you back!   *Jane*

★ ★ ★

Horrible habits

We have four toilets in our house – three upstairs
and one downstairs. The downstairs toilet is right by
the front door, so it seems like common sense to me
not to do a poo in it, because if someone then comes
to the door it's embarrassing!! Okay, if we didn't
have three toilets upstairs, but we do. So why can't
my husband get it into his head? Sometimes he tries
to sneak in when I'm not looking and I say, 'How
long is it going to take you to go upstairs and do a
poo in one of the three toilets up there?' *Denise*

I think men should get penalty points on
their licence for leaving towels on the bed
and the loo seat up. They'd have to make
up for it . . . in other ways!!! *Andrea*

☆☆ ☆☆ ☆☆ ☆☆

You don't mind washing somebody's underwear when you're in love with them, but when you fall out of love, you think, 'What's that?'
Sherrie

☆☆ ☆☆ ☆☆ ☆☆

Isn't it funny how, when you first meet someone, even if they eat like a pig and they've got manky feet, you think, I love that about him! I love his manky feet. Then, as soon as you fall out of love with them, you think, 'You revolting person!' *Coleen*

* * *

Men are like dogs

Men need training. You should tell them how to do things, how to make you enjoy life and have a good time. They don't know. If they weren't doing something properly, I'd say, 'Get a grip or I'm leaving!' But what would they get a grip of?   *Sherrie*

A word of praise will do an awful lot more for a man's ego than a word of criticism. A kind word will get a lot more out of someone than a harsh one. You've got to nurture as well as nag.   *Jane*

☆☆ ☆☆ ☆☆ ☆☆

If you want to do something, first plant the idea in the man's head. Then he thinks it's his idea, which means you get to do it.

Lesley

☆☆ ☆☆ ☆☆ ☆☆

If you don't tell men what to do, they don't do it; if you tell them, they call you a nag. You can't win! On the other hand, they're damned if they do and they're damned if they don't. If they've emptied the dryer, they've done it wrong; if they haven't, why didn't they? *Coleen*

Living with Steve is like learning to live with a great big dog. Of course, living with a great big dog is brilliant, because it adds a lot to your family. But you can't be as anal as you were before, because you'll just be shouting at the dog a lot and that's just going to ruin everybody's day. *Andrea*

* * *

Men are from Mars . . .

I often wonder where men put everything. There must be compartments, or separate drawers. Where does it all fit? Because there are a lot of things going on down there, aren't there? *Sherrie*

☆☆ ☆☆ ☆☆ ☆☆

A recent report found that apparently men are 'more predictable' than women. They call that news?

Kate

☆☆ ☆☆ ☆☆ ☆☆

I think women live a lot more in their imaginations than men do. We fantasise a lot more. We dream a lot more. That's why we're more spontaneous than men. *Lesley*

Men are lovely. We've got to agree on that. We love them all. *Jane*

I like a bit of spontaneity. My husband used to be very spontaneous. The most spontaneous thing he did was marry me. It happened in a nanosecond. We met and we were off. I looked at my watch and I'd had two kids! He's got a little more predictable as he's got older.

Is it predictable, though – or is it dependable? My husband is lovely and very dependable, but I wouldn't half mind him saying to me, 'Come on, love. Let's chuck in the jobs and take a camper van round North America.' Part of me just longs to do that. *Lesley*

I have met men and, the split second I've met them, I've thought, 'You're horrible!' You would never be friends with a woman who was horrible, would you? So why would you go on a date with a man who was horrible and then expect him to be nice to you? *Andrea*

The great thing about men is that they like different things in different women, because we'd be in a sorry state if they all wanted the same thing. *Jane*

Men have a one-track mind. They're only able to think about one thing at a time. When they drive, they drive. When we drive, we're cooking, washing, cleaning, looking after the kids, making the dinner, putting our make-up on *and* driving.   *Sherrie*

Men are like buses: it doesn't matter if you miss one because there's always another behind him.   *Jane*

★ ★ ★

Man flu

Man flu seriously gets on my nerves. I have to bite my tongue, though. It's not worth getting into a fight about, because in their head they're dying and you know they're not!   *Andrea*

Have you noticed how men clutch the furniture when they walk in the room, just in case they pass out? When all they've got is a cold?   *Denise*

When you have real flu, your head's pounding, you're sweating, you're freezing one minute and boiling hot the next and you can't move. So when people say, 'Argh, I've got such bad flu,' I say, 'You haven't! Just be realistic about what's wrong with you!' It really winds me up. *Carol*

My husband gets man flu. If he gets a
runny nose it's like, 'I've got the flu.'
And I think, 'No love, you've got a runny nose: now
get up and put the bins out.' I'm sympathetic up to
a point. Initially I'll say, 'Do you feel bad? Do you
want a Beecham's or a cup of tea?' But after a couple
of hours I say, 'Do you want a smack in the gob?
Because you are getting on my nerves now.' *Coleen*

Men in dressing gowns either look like Hugh
Hefner or your granddad, don't they? *Carol*

★ ★ ★

Dream man

We're not perfect but if, overall, you're good, understanding and good-humoured, you're getting there. What makes the ideal man? It's the same thing that makes an ideal woman really, just being a good person.   *Andrea*

☆☆ ☆☆ ☆☆ ☆☆

I don't think there is an ideal man, because nobody's perfect. Everyone's got bad habits and everyone's a bit annoying at times. We're human beings. We're flawed.
Carol

☆☆ ☆☆ ☆☆ ☆☆

Women fall for the wrong man because they're looking at an idealised version of the bloke; they're seeing what they want to see rather than what's standing in front of them.   *Andrea*

179

☆☆ ☆☆ ☆☆ ☆☆

One of the best life mottoes I ever heard was
from Maya Angelou: 'When somebody shows
you who they are, believe them.' I wish somebody
had told me that when I was a lot younger.
When you're younger and it comes to the opposite
sex, you often think you can change people, or
they've got potential. You're not really paying
attention to the behaviour in front of you, or
how the person is. You're just seeing what you're
looking for and what you'd like them to be like.
Now, in all areas of my life, I judge people
on what they present to me. I think that's
probably a far less painful way to go through
life than judging people on who you think
they might be, given half a chance. *Jane*

☆☆ ☆☆ ☆☆ ☆☆

Roxanne was gutted to find Dave looked nothing like his picture on the internet dating site. And he definitely wasn't 6'2" either!

Work

☆ ☆ ☆

Now, the theory goes that the twenty-first-century woman can have it all. She can have a lovely husband, family, friends and a glittering career, and still have time to exercise three times a week and write a novel in her spare time. As we all know, things don't really work like that in the real world, and sadly 'having it all' can translate into just plain 'doing it all' if you're not too careful. Whether you're banging your head on the glass ceiling or defending your right to be a stay-at-home mum, we hope that these pearls of wisdom inspire you to keep on keeping on.

* * *

Equal rights?

I'm so glad we live in today's world, because I would have hated to live in my grandmother's world, and even my mother's world, up to a point, where women were just the secondary earners and went out and did a little bit of part-time, just to fit in with the kids. But now that women have careers – as a woman without children – I'm so glad I've got that choice. *Jane*

It's a really good thing if the glass ceiling, whatever that is, has been smashed. Women are getting into boardroom jobs, but that's probably only because they're really good and better than any man who's applied for it. *Carol*

Who will be there with the dustpan and brush to clear up the mess once women smash the glass ceiling? *Lynda*

* * *

Having it all

Feminism has meant that women have too many choices. A lot of women are now under terrible pressure to take all of those choices and do everything and have everything at once, which is completely wrong. If you try to have it all, something will always suffer.   *Carol*

The work/life balance needs to be developed through legislation and it's beginning to take off. Employers have to allow for both men and women to bring up families. We have an awful lot of children with no parents at home.   *Lynda*

I think women are being more honest about what they really want these days. Quite a few women admit, 'I want to be at home with my kids. I want to be a housewife.' They're not ashamed to say it, whereas they used to be.   *Carol*

Women are a nightmare. We're never happy with what we're doing. When I was working on *GMTV* and *Loose Women*,

I was never happy where I was. If I was at home, I'd think, 'Oh dear, I shouldn't be at home, I should be trying harder at work.' If I was at home, I'd think, 'I should be at work.' It means that no matter what foot you've got in which camp, you're never happy. That's not necessarily feminism's fault; it's something to do with the way women think. *Andrea*

☆☆ ☆☆ ☆☆ ☆☆

Frankly, I would feel safer in this world if it were run by women. There would be fewer wars if women ran the world. That's a fact.
Carol

☆☆ ☆☆ ☆☆ ☆☆

Really? At certain times of the month I could eat children raw. If I were in charge of a button that could blow everybody up and I'd just had an argument with the boyfriend or something, I would probably press the button and say, 'There! You can take that as well!' *Jane*

How to be a Domestic Goddess

☆ ☆ ☆

Well, they say an Englishman's home is his castle. What they don't say is that it's also his dumping ground, the place where he can surround himself with old newspapers and boxes of half-eaten pizza. And that's where we, unfortunately, seem to come in. Some women delight in doing a Nigella – keeping a house in perfect order and a kitchen bubbling over while always looking good enough to eat. Others are more sluttish – shoving clutter into cupboards and turning down the lights when friends and family come round. Whether you're a saint or a sinner, we're sure these domestic confessions will strike a chord.

★ ★ ★

Domestic Goddess? Eat your heart out, Nigella.

How clean is your house?

I used to do it all: the cooking, the cleaning, the washing, the ironing, and it's all a load of old trollocks! *Sherrie*

I love cooking and I love creating a homely environment. When people say that women shouldn't take on these stereotypical roles, I don't quite understand it, because I get such pleasure from seeing people sit round my table, or come home to a cup of tea and a piece of toast. *Lynda*

☆☆ ☆☆ ☆☆ ☆☆

I can't cook and I don't want to learn because then I'd have to do it!

Denise

☆☆ ☆☆ ☆☆ ☆☆

Man about the house

It seems that scientists – or 'researchers' – have found the perfect excuse for men to get out of doing the housework. A study, conducted by a man I might add, has found that household chores, including using a vacuum cleaner or a microwave oven, could reduce a man's chance of having children by lowering his sperm count. Yeah, right, and I'm Dolly Parton! *Kate*

☆☆ ☆☆ ☆☆ ☆☆

If a man does the vacuuming, the hoover has to be left in the middle of the floor, just in case you miss it when you come in!

Denise

☆☆ ☆☆ ☆☆ ☆☆

You have to train men to be domestic, God love 'em. I work as hard as my other half and I wouldn't expect to go and clean his house just as I wouldn't expect him to come and clean mine. My mother cleans mine, obviously! *Jane*

I'm always saying to Ray, 'Don't die, because I don't know how to do my tax return.' At the same time, he's saying, 'Don't die, because I don't know where Ciara's uniform is.' We each have our jobs and we do them! *Coleen*

I like a man who does a bit of cleaning. I find it really attractive. I've said it before: I like a man in a pinny. Nothing else, just a pinny! *Zoe*

Sandra had a thorough clean out before the garage sale. She was planning to give away her mother-in-law with the rug in a special BOGOF promotion.

Holidays

☆ ☆ ☆

Most of us have a fantasy about what our perfect holiday would be like. We'd pack a simple, stylish capsule wardrobe in a tiny bag, sleep all the way there and arrive to perfect sunshine every day. Lounging by the pool, we'd work on our tan while our significant other fetched us drinks, looking remarkably like Daniel Craig in his little swim trunks. Either that, or there'd be dozens of handsome men to flirt with over tropical cocktails. This fantasy is so appealing because it edits out a few things: noisy kids, mosquitoes, sunburn, jet lag, and the fact that your fella in budgie smugglers just ain't licensed to thrill. Here's how we see it . . .

★ ★ ★

Dream get-away?

I like a good cruise, me.   *Jane*

I used to love going on holiday on my own. I like the feeling of solitude. Almost all my life I've had to talk for a living, so it's great to say nothing for a while.   *Carol*

I love going to hot places, but there's always one drawback. Mosquitoes! You're lying on the beach or by the pool and the tan is coming along a treat and you hear a buzz and you think, 'Don't you dare bite me!!!'   *Lynda*

Normally, I have to come home from holiday because my liver drags me screaming onto the aircraft. 'No, I don't want to go!' I'll say. 'Yeah, we're going,' it replies. So I have to come home otherwise I'd die.   *Carol*

★ ★ ★

'Yes,' thought Melinda happily, as she looked over at Stavros, 'I can see what the appeal of a *package* holiday is...'

Holiday romance

I haven't had a holiday romance for a long time, but when
I was in my twenties, I had some kind of romance every
time I went on holiday. It just made the trip more interesting and fun. My friends and I used to think, 'Where
can we go where we can get off with boys?'   *Carol*

It's difficult when you're buying trunks for your fella. I went to
buy some the other day and I'm thinking, Daniel Craig coming
out of the sea. But when he put them on, I said, 'Oh no, love,
no.' They needed some netting in the bottom. He needed
a bit more support than Daniel Craig had on his!   *Jane*

☆☆ ☆☆ ☆☆ ☆☆

You know what they call those small Speedo type swimming trunks? Budgie smugglers!
Carol

☆☆ ☆☆ ☆☆ ☆☆

Travel 101

When I was twenty-two, I backpacked around the world for a year. I set off with so much stuff: curling tongs, about twenty pairs of knickers, three towels (one for my hair, one for my body and one for the beach). After three days in India I realised what a mistake I'd made and got rid of it all. Ever since then I've made sure I don't over-pack. *Andrea*

People make such a great fuss over long-distance travel, but it's not difficult really. You can have a few drinks, or maybe take a sleeping tablet, and wake up having had a lovely night's sleep. (Also, if the plane crashes, you won't know anything about it!) *Carol*

If they could invent family-only planes where all hell could break loose and no one would care, I think they would do very well. It would be so great to know that they're going to have nappies and milk on

the plane, or colouring books, and the air steward-
esses aren't going to look at you like you're something they've trodden in because your child is
screaming and refuses to sit down.   *Andrea*

The Mysteries of Modern Britain

☆ ☆ ☆

Well, we like to think of ourselves as smart women (at least most of the time!) but there are just some things we can never get our heads round, and we're sure we're not alone here. There's modern technology that's supposed to make life easier, but that just ends up driving us round the bend. There are hardworking people like teachers and doctors who never seem to get the credit they deserve. And then there's Twitter. What's that about then? We on *Loose Women* like to tell it like it is, so read on for a list of our pet gripes about life in twenty-first-century Britain.

★ ★ ★

Nigel, the Health and Safety officer, had
deemed the playground 'a death trap'.

The state of the nation

What we need is hope. We need a leader; we need the British spirit back; we need to get off our bums and get out there. We need somebody who's going to lift us right up and give us hope. If they keep saying it's doom, we'll all go down. *Sherrie*

Who doesn't complain about the state of public transport in this country? Everybody does and everybody has a right to, because it's disgusting. It's too expensive, it doesn't work, it's filthy, you can't get a seat, it doesn't work and it's late; where do you want me to start? *Carol*

Education is the most important thing in our country. To me, it's so important, it's almost sacred. I can't understand anyone who would knock the principle of our society becoming better educated. It has got to be a good thing. Education has been an incredibly important part of my own life, because my parents were both railway workers when I was a kid. My dad was a signalman and my mum was in the ticket office, and they decided that they wanted to become more highly educated and improve their lives. They worked really hard at night school, they got the qualifications and went to teacher training college – all while my sisters and I were little. They managed to get grants and my father ended up as a headmaster by the time I was twelve. Mum was head of music in the middle school. They could not have done that without the incredible education facilities that were available then and which are even better now. *Lesley*

* * *

Little mysteries

Algebra. Who needs it? *Jane*

Why is it either too hot or too cold all the time? I don't know why it's so difficult to get the temperature right inside. *Carol*

Why is it that some dogs end up looking just like their owners?

Why do you need an explanation for life going
wrong? Life just does go wrong sometimes. *Jane*

* * *

Bête noirs

I try to get away with just one kiss when I greet people,
because I find two kisses so boring, even though it probably started as a showbizzy thing. I certainly couldn't be
doing with three. Three kisses is ridiculous! *Denise*

I can't imagine anything worse than speed dating! What's the
point of going into a room and talking to someone for three
minutes? It's not all that different to going to one of the bars
in Bangkok and just picking someone off the stage. *Carol*

It makes me apoplectic when I see doctors
criticised in the press, because they're the
hardest-working people I know. *Lesley*

I get annoyed with those women who say, 'I'm equal! Treat me like an equal! But you earn the money and I'll spend it.' That's not equality, is it? You've got to go for the whole deal.   *Lynda*

☆☆ ☆☆ ☆☆ ☆☆

I don't see the point in spending a lot of money on toilet paper. I can get four rolls for 40p in my local shop. Since all I'm going to do with it is throw it down the toilet, what's the point in spending £2 on it?
Carol

☆☆ ☆☆ ☆☆ ☆☆

Why would you wear an animal fur on your back when it should be on the animal?   *Sherrie*

★ ★ ★

Motoring madness

Why do bus lane restriction times keep changing? First they're 24 hours, the next minute it's 9–4, and then it's 4–5, so you keep straying into them and then you get done! It's extortion. It's about getting money out of you.   *Carol*

The M25 – all those lanes and it's still a car park!   *Lynda*

I understand that women with babies in the back need a bit more space in car parks, but why do they have to have the spaces right near the lift, or right near the store? They're not disabled. They can walk from over there the same way I have to.   *Carol*

* * *

It's good to talk

There's a clue in the name: mobile phones. When people don't answer the phone or they don't call you back for days, they say,

'I didn't have my mobile phone with me.' It's a mobile phone. That's what you're supposed to do. Take it with you.   *Carol*

I love Twitter. Don't diss the Twit!   *Carol*

When I answer the phone and my grandson Ollie is asleep, I whisper, 'Hi.' They whisper, 'Hi,' back. I say, 'No, *you* don't need to whisper!'   *Sherrie*

The thing that really gets me about call centres is that when you finally get to speak to a person, they're in another country. They don't know that it's snowing in Muswell Hill and I'm feeling very grumpy and I've just got a parking fine! 'Where are you?' I asked one of them the other day. 'I'm in Capetown,' she said. 'Well, exactly!'   *Lynda*

I love the Internet! I don't know what I'd do all day without it. It's important to me, but I do think it's beginning to take over people's lives. When you think about it, we still managed when we didn't have any of that stuff. We still managed with one phone on a little table in the hall, next to the phone book.   *Carol*

* * *

Kids these days . . .

It's a bit intimidating on Halloween when a six-foot teen-ager turns up with a Scream mask on. You think, 'Is he here to trick or treat, or is he going to mug me?' *Jane*

The thing that annoys me about all the girls who are photo-graphed kissing each other is that they do it because they know they're going to have their photographs taken. It's a very cynical ploy on their part. In my day, we did it quietly at school behind closed doors, to practise snogging. *Lynda*

I don't understand why girls wear big furry boots in the summer when it's boiling hot: short skirts, a little T-shirt, no tights and then a big fat woolly pair of boots. What's that all about, then? *Coleen*

Behaving Badly

☆ ☆ ☆

Now, when it comes to bad behaviour rest assured that we know what we're talking about. We'd be the first to admit that we're no angels, but then who is? From where we're sitting, there's enough toilet humour, lairy behaviour and effing and blinding going on to fill a book the size of a telephone directory – and that's just the women! And then there's the more subtle bad behaviour, like the people who flirt with your other half the minute your back is turned. Well, this is our chance to let off some stream . . . and maybe make a few confessions of our own.

* * *

Effing and blinding

I swear like a trooper, but I swear with people I'm comfortable with and have known for a long time. If I walk into
a room and within ten minutes, there's a woman standing there swearing loudly, I immediately think, 'Oh,
nice, lady.' But it's all right if a bloke's doing it, because
you expect men to be common, horrible pigs!   *Coleen*

Sometimes, there's only one thing to do, and that's swear!   *Lynda*

Cookery programmes are the worst for swearing, aren't
they? I'm somebody who enjoys a good swear, but I
don't like to hear it on the television when they're telling you how to make a goat's cheese tartlet.   *Denise*

Swearing loses its effectiveness when it becomes
too commonplace. We need a new word,
because the rest are all worn out.   *Carol*

* * *

Deal-breakers

I had a partner who used to walk five paces in front of me, because I always had stilettos on and couldn't keep up. He was totally oblivious that I was there. He just left me behind. I could have been kidnapped or anything. I just don't think he liked me! *Jane*

If I was going out with someone and he walked into the garage on Christmas Eve, picked something up, wrapped it and said, 'Er, here you go,' that would be it for me. I can't stand that lack of effort. He'd be out the door. *Carol*

I still find it hard to believe that people will try and pull the wool over your eyes and tell you things that are completely untrue, simply for their own gain. *Jane*

★ ★ ★

Bad girls

☆☆ ☆☆ ☆☆ ☆☆

I'm not as bad as people think. I've done some bad things in my time. I've tried a few things that I probably shouldn't have, but I'm not a bad girl, really, generally, sometimes, maybe . . .

Carol

☆☆ ☆☆ ☆☆ ☆☆

I certainly don't drink enough water. I hate that pressure to drink water. I'd always rather have a cup of tea, or a vodka! *Denise*

I've always said it: we all make mistakes because we're human beings. *Coleen*

I really love the sound of blow-offs, farts! It's always so absolutely hilarious. Don't tell me you've never laughed when somebody's done a really loud blow-off? *Carol*

I'm usually very placid and happy. But, by God, I've got a vicious temper if somebody attacks me or mine. You might not think that about me, but it's true. I'm very good at defending myself. I'll try to do it with wit and humour first. But if I'm not getting the point across, then I will definitely shout. *Jane*

* * *

Getting an eye-full

I was in a nightclub in Ibiza once, a complete innocent abroad. I noticed a crowd had congregated and they were all looking up. 'What's going on?' I thought. It wasn't a kinky club; it was a proper club, but the theme of the night was 'naughty'. I looked up to see a couple suspended in a net above me, *doing it*. All I could see was his party bag! It was arguably the most un-erotic, unattractive, disgusting thing I've ever seen and you couldn't have got me in a cab quick enough!   *Kate*

If I were to live one night over and over again, I think it would be the night I was at G-A-Y judging a porn idol competition. Naked men stripping, brilliant. No, seriously. Actually, yes, seriously!   *Carol*

There's nothing more intimidating for a man than to be ogled at by a group of women shouting, 'Hiya, get your kit off!' We're quite scary at times!   *Zoe*

Women are programmed to crotch watch, whether you like it or not. I watched a documentary, where they used lasers and sensors and showed women pictures of men and men pictures of women. The men looked at women's chests and the women looked at men's crotches. But they denied it, because they didn't know they were doing it. Denise Welch is the only woman I know who admits it. When she meets a bloke, the first thing she looks at is the crotch!   *Carol*

* * *

Inappropriate flirting

Flirting is a waste of time. It's so disrespectful and rude when people in relationships flirt with other people. It makes me very, very cross. People who say it's OK are completely wrong.   *Carol*

A couple of times a friend's partner has been just a little bit too fresh or tactile with me, or they've said something like, 'You know, I've always really liked you.' In response, I've said, 'You don't really mean that, do you? Because if you say something like that, you're going to get into really big trouble, because I'm going to go and tell her.' I would always deal with it then and there. I wouldn't take the problem and then multiply it by a million by going to her and saying, 'Do you know what he did?'   *Lisa*

I've been in the situation where women have hit on my ex-husband and yes, he did succumb. But I also know that they pushed it and pushed it and I blame them just as much, for having the gall to go after him.   *Sherrie*

☆☆ ☆☆ ☆☆ ☆☆

Women always blame other women for everything. It's never the guy who gets all the crap; it's always the other woman. I find that strange.
Carol

☆☆ ☆☆ ☆☆ ☆☆

Behaving Well

☆ ☆ ☆

Well, even Loose Women know when they have to mind their Ps and Qs. Just because we like to have a good time doesn't mean that we don't buckle down when it really matters, or that we don't appreciate old-fashioned values like friendship, tolerance and honesty. Having said that, even honesty should have its limits. Telling a friend that you don't like her expensive new haircut, for example, is a big 'no no' in our books. I mean, have you ever honestly thanked someone for pointing out that your bum really does look big in that dress?

* * *

Big picture

Sometimes you have to put right your wrongs. It's the right thing to do, the decent thing to do, rather than bolting, without looking back. I can't bear a runner. *Kate*

Everybody's entitled to believe whatever they want and not be judged for it. *Carol*

It's a sign of strength to go and see a therapist, if you care enough and you've got to the point where you can't sort something out yourself. *Lisa*

I'm not a particularly religious person and I'm not entirely sure that there's going to be another life after this. So I'm not going to give things up in this life because of what might happen in the next. I'm still nice to people; I still do a lot for my charities; I'm still a good person, or try to be. But I can be naughty if I want to! *Denise*

* * *

Vice and virtues

When I'm in a situation with a lot of people I
don't know, I'm well behaved and I know when I
have to go to bed, but when I'm with Mark and
my friends it's completely different.   *Carol*

☆☆ ☆☆ ☆☆ ☆☆

**I'm trying to give up smoking. Or at
least, I've got as far as carrying Nicorette
patches in my handbag next to my
cigarettes. It is a start, isn't it?
I'm mentally preparing myself.**

Coleen

☆☆ ☆☆ ☆☆ ☆☆

I'm a real backseat driver and I can't help myself. I've tried:
I've even put my fist in my mouth. Being someone who has
been on the other end of being criticised constantly, I'm a

little more forgiving now. So I tend to stand back a bit and count to ten before I say, 'Stop! We're going to die!' *Jane*

At the beginning of a relationship, we all pretend that we don't go to the toilet. If you're in a hotel room, you go for a wee down the side of the bowl. You certainly never do a (whisper) Number Two! You give yourself tummy aches and all sorts of things, because you pretend you never go. *Denise*

★ ★ ★

Tolerance is golden

Belle de Jour said that all a man wants is complete acceptance and I really get her point. My Paul is the same. He would like me to be by his side. Sometimes when a man feels like the world's on his shoulders and everybody is judging him, he just wants you, as his lady, to say, 'I don't care what anybody says. I think

220

you're great.' But if I think he's wrong, I can't do it!!!
I think that to stand by your man is the right thing
to do, so I wish I could keep my gob shut!   *Lisa*

No one has any right to tell anybody what they can
wear. It doesn't matter if it's fur, a burkha or a tracksuit and trainers. Who is to judge people for what
they wear? I find it really bizarre.   *Carol*

☆☆ ☆☆ ☆☆ ☆☆

**You can't like everybody and not
everybody's going to like you. So as long
as you remember that, it's fine.**

Jane

☆☆ ☆☆ ☆☆ ☆☆

If you're going to be tolerant, you've got to be tolerant of everything. You can't pick and choose what
you're tolerant of. I am very tolerant and I think it's

a little bit unequal in this country, because there are
certain things that are tolerated more than others,
especially when it comes to religion.   *Carol*

★ ★ ★

Little white lies

I would never say to a friend, 'Oh, you look atro-
cious in that!' I'd get round it by saying, 'I
prefer you in that other outfit; I think you
look fabulous in the other one.'   *Jane*

Women don't want the real answer to the question,
'Does my bum look big in this?' It doesn't matter if
they're asking you, the boyfriend or the husband, they
want you to say, 'No, you look fine!' If you say, 'Actually,
it looks massive,' it would start an argument. People can't
handle the truth, so they just shouldn't ask.   *Carol*

If I knew someone who was unhappy because they felt they were overweight, I would probably come up with some suggestions to try to help them find a way of losing weight. It wouldn't necessarily be by saying, 'Stop stuffing your face and get down the gym.' It would be more like, 'Look if it's really getting you down, then I can find out about some classes you can do and a really good way of helping you lose the weight.' I wouldn't have a problem being honest with somebody.   *Lisa*

I would never open a present and say, 'Oh my God, that is awful!' not even to my husband, and I would hope that he would never do that to me. I'm brilliant at pretending I like something. Perhaps, a couple of days later, I might change it quietly. My husband would never know if I wore it anyway: he doesn't pay that much attention!   *Coleen*

Put-Downs and Compliments

☆ ☆ ☆

There's nothing that can lift your day like a compliment, even if it is just a wolf-whistle and an 'Alright, gorgeous!' as you walk past a building site. When we were younger we might have rolled our eyes and tutted, but these days we take what we can get! But of course, it cuts both ways. The right words can make you feel like a million dollars, but they can also cut someone down to size, pretty quickly. Since we're a mouthy lot, we'll leave you with this selection of our all-time favourite zingers. Happy reading!

★ ★ ★

Sticks and stones . . .

☆☆ ☆☆ ☆☆ ☆☆

I was doing this play in the West End and somebody came up after the first night and said, 'Lynda, you looked fantastic!' My ex-husband said, 'Yes, she's very good from a distance, my wife.'
Lynda

☆☆ ☆☆ ☆☆ ☆☆

I started worrying about wrinkles when I first got married. My husband said to me, 'You're getting a bit old look-ing.' I was thirty-three! He also used to go on about my weight quite a lot. It never leaves you after that, does it? Up until then, I was quite happy with myself.   *Jane*

I was going out with a really lovely bloke; he was really nice, but I just didn't want to go out with him anymore. I was young and I couldn't bring myself to say the words. He popped out for something and I wrote on a napkin the first letters of the words, 'I don't want to go out with you anymore.' I-D-W-T-G-O-W-Y-A. Then I put, 'Work it out,' and left!   *Carol*

There's no nice way to dump someone. I just can't turn round to a man and say, 'Look, love, I don't fancy you. You're ugly and your breath smells.' I was once in a bar with someone and I thought, 'Oh, I don't fancy you!' 'I'm just going to the ladies,' I said, and I never came back.   *Coleen*

☆☆ ☆☆ ☆☆ ☆☆

I put down my ex once in the throes of passion. 'Can't you think of anybody, either?' I said.

Jane

☆☆ ☆☆ ☆☆ ☆☆

Pet peeves

If someone turned round to me and said, 'Zoe, just chil-
lax!' I'd want to punch them. I just think it's a stupid,
pathetic, ridiculous, childish word. I tell you what
I really hate, what makes me want to throw things
during an argument, is when someone says, 'Yeah,
yeah, yeah,' over me when I'm speaking.   *Zoe*

The word I hate the most is very, very small. It's
'if'. When Steve and I are having a row and he
says, 'All right, I'm sorry if you thought that I was
being out of line.' That little if! He doesn't say, 'I'm
sorry, I was being out of order.' It's, 'Sorry IF you
thought I was being out of order.'   *Andrea*

★ ★ ★

Flattery will get you everywhere

☆☆ ☆☆ ☆☆ ☆☆

Men have to pay you compliments. Obviously, Tim does it all the time, because he thinks that's the only way he'll get any jiggy-jigs! It doesn't work, though.

Denise

☆☆ ☆☆ ☆☆ ☆☆

If I say to Ray, 'I love you,' he'll reply, 'Shut up, you idiot!' I know now, after nine years of being together, that it means, 'I love you too.' He's a stereotypical Yorkshire man!　*Coleen*

I think most people are quite flattered to be asked where they bought something. I'll ask anybody, whether I know them or not. I'd be so thrilled if someone asked me where my clothes were from that I'd probably take them down to the shop and have lunch with them!　*Andrea*

If somebody says I'm nice, I'm very flattered. Nice is a step up from 'You're all right.' Nice is a nice thing to be. *Jane*

Nice is a mamby pamby pimby wimby
womby wamby word! *Sherrie*

☆☆ ☆☆ ☆☆ ☆☆

I like the word Phwoooar! It's so much better than 'Cor'. Sometimes you don't need to say anything else.

Carol

☆☆ ☆☆ ☆☆ ☆☆

The end

We hope you've enjoyed our Little Book! We had a great time putting it together and lots of chuckles looking back on some of the more outrageous things we've said . . .

We hope there have been a few pearls of wisdom that you might find useful, and that you had a belly full of laughs along the way!

Love the Loose Women xx

Acknowledgements

Following the success of our first two books *Girls' Night In* and *Here Come the Girls!* it has been a real pleasure to produce this book of our words of wisdom and anecdotes. Once again a big thank you needs to go to our writer Rebecca Cripps for compiling our many stories & thoughts.

We would also like to thank the Loose Women production team who have worked on *The Little Book of Loose Women*; in particular Fiona Keenaghan, Karl Newton, Donna Gower and Emily Humphries.

Last but not least, every good book needs a great publisher and we have been very lucky once again to have had the incredible support and talents of Hodder & Stoughton, in particular our editor Fenella Bates and her team Ciara Foley, Sarah Christie and Susan Spratt.